A Bridge to Independence

The Kent Family Placement Project

NANCY HAZEL

Basil Blackwell · Oxford

First published in 1981 by
Basil Blackwell Publisher
108 Cowley Road
Oxford OX4 1JF
England

British Library Cataloguing in Publication Data

Hazel, Nancy
    A bridge to independence. – (Practice of social
    work; 9).
    1. Adolescence   2. Foster home care – England –
    Kent
    I. Title   II. Series
    362.7'33'094223   HV887.G72K/

    ISBN 0–631–12943–X
    ISBN 0–631–12596–5 Pbk

Photoset by Nene Phototypesetters Ltd, Northampton
Printed in Great Britain by
The Blackwell Press Ltd
Guildford, London, Oxford, Worcester

A BRIDGE TO INDEPENDENCE

The Practice of Social Work

General editors: Bill Jordan and Jean Packman

Contents

Acknowledgements

This book has been put together by a team of people – the project social workers and secretaries, the project families and adolescents, and members of the Kent Social Services Department, although I have acted as editor and have written parts of it myself.

However, it was Nicolas Stacey, Director of Social Services, Kent County Council, who brought the scheme to life by believing in it and by persuading the Gatsby Charitable Foundation to give it generous financial backing. Vic George, Professor of Social Work and Social Administration at the University of Kent, Mary Jobbins, Social Work Service Officer, Department of Health and Social Security, and Jane Rowe, at that time Director of the Association of British Adoption and Fostering Agencies, gave unfaltering support throughout the five years of the project's life. Roger Morgan and his successor, Mike Lauerman, research officers to the Kent Department of Social Services, also gave a great deal of help. Perhaps the hardest task fell to Leslie Sheppard, Assistant Director, Personnel and Research, who acted as the link between the project and the Department, resolving problems and ironing out difficulties with a quiet persistence that was almost always successful.

The project team consisted of five social workers and four secretaries. The social workers were Rosemary Tozer (joined May 1975 and left to have a baby in May 1979); Peter Ashley-Mudie (joined January 1976); Jeremy Roberts (joined September 1977); Pam Harris (joined May 1979); Roger Meekings (joined August 1979). The secretaries were: Sue Hodgman (joined February 1975 and left to have a baby in November 1976); Julia Geeves (part-time from February 1976); Linda Hoskins (joined March 1977 and left to have a baby in October 1977); Tina Lewis (joined January 1978). The only reason for which anyone left the team during the project was pregnancy. It was a very stable and close-knit group, and I should like to say how much I enjoyed our friendship and collaboration throughout the project's life. I am especially grateful to Julia Geeves for typing and checking the manuscripts.

It was also particularly rewarding to work together with the foster-families on a team basis, and their contributions to this book speak for themselves. With some reluctance, where adolescents and families are referred to in the text all names and identifying data have been changed, as it might not always be agreeable to the people concerned to be easily recognized.

Finally, special thanks to the boys and girls who demonstrated for us how resilient and adaptable young people can be.

Nancy Hazel

1 A New Kind of Foster Care: The Kent Demonstration Project

Social work education and research is a substantial and costly industry, but it is one in which consumer satisfaction with the product is consistently lacking. There appears to be a constant gap between social work teachers and the theory they teach, and the tasks which face social workers each day in their environment-modifying, people-changing activities. Similarly, research (even research of impeccable quality that attracts considerable critical acclaim) may have virtually no impact on practice. For example, family placement – which affects radically the lives of almost half the children in public care – has been almost untaught on social work courses,[1] and George's careful study of fostering,[2] with its far-sighted recommendations, did not change practice at all.

The Kent project sought to link theory and practice, to illustrate a new way of placing adolescents and to prove that this method was successful. From the outset everything was to be made as explicit as possible, so that it could be seen whether both the basic theory and the chosen methods stood the test of practice. In fact, the original blueprint was never changed, and the scheme has been rather successful. It also seems as if this very practical piece of research *has* managed to produce changes in current social work practice.

It was intended that the Kent project should be both an innovatory social work enterprise and a piece of research; it was described as a demonstration project. The scheme was an attempt to discover whether it is possible or desirable for England[3] to develop a community-based placement policy – an attempt, in other words, to show that adolescents with severe problems, who would formerly have been considered 'unsuitable for fostering', could be placed and maintained in families in the community and that these placements could reduce or solve their problems. Specifically, the questions that the project tried to answer were those outlined in its first *Annual Report*:

> If you spend as much money on developing a family placement in the community as it costs to use a residential place, can you obtain more effective help for the adolescent with severe problems who must, *unavoidably*, leave his home, at any rate for a short period?
> Can ordinary people, in their own homes, provide *effective* help to teenagers with severe problems?
> If help can be given in this way, are there some adolescents who cannot profit by it? If so, which?

The scheme was a research project in that it was committed to describing and evaluating the work for publication.

Following negotiations carried out by Nicolas Stacey, Director of Social Services for Kent County Council, in June 1974 agreement was reached in principle that the Gatsby Charitable Foundation, the Kent Social Services Department and the University of Kent should collaborate in a five-year experimental project to test out how far the functions at present performed by residential institutions for children and young persons could be transferred to persons living in private homes in the community. I was appointed organizer of the project, with the status of Senior Research Fellow of the University of Kent. My salary was paid by the Gatsby Charitable Foundation, and the running expenses of the project were met by Kent Social Services Committee. The staff of the project included a senior social worker and a secretary, whose salaries were paid by the Foundation.

The Social Services Committee agreed to a weekly payment to the foster-parents up to a maximum of £50 (the minimum cost of a place in a residential institution, but less than the cost of a place in a residential centre for adolescents with problems). Throughout the five years of the project the support and encouragement given by members of the Committee never wavered.

In the autumn of 1974 I wrote the following preliminary definition of the scheme, setting out its objectives and our justification for choosing this particular field of action.

The functions of residential establishments have been defined as:

(1) Reception/shelter
(2) Observation/classification/diagnosis
(3) Substitute home care – short/long-term
(4) Treatment – short/long-term
(5) Custodial.

These terms are fairly self-explanatory except for treatment, which appears to have two meanings:

(a) Any defined programme of care or help
(b) A specifically 'therapeutic' approach.

For the project's purposes 'treatment' was held to mean any defined programme of care or help with the goal of producing changes likely to improve the child or young person's ability to live in society.

It would appear theoretically possible to transfer all five functions to families or family-sized units, provided the principles of paying high fees for difficult and skilled tasks was accepted.

However, a small demonstration project must define realistic objectives. It was, therefore, proposed not to conduct any trials with (1) Reception/shelter, or (5) Custody, in both of which the issue of security is highly significant. It was proposed to exclude (2) Assessment, on the grounds that to shift this function into the community means re-routing a number of services (medical, psychological, etc.). It was proposed to exclude (3) Substitute home care, on the grounds that placements of this kind are relatively well-understood and widely practised.

'Treatment' was, therefore, the chosen target and the scheme was to be restricted to older age groups (over 10). Such a choice appeared to be justified for various reasons:

(1) During the period from 1960 to 1972 the age group 15–17 showed the most rapid rise among the children in care. Other age groups showed either a modest rise (5–15) or a decline (under 5).

(2) The number of long-stay children under Section 1 dropped rapidly, but the number of care orders increased sharply. [Section 1 of the Children Act 1948 deals with

voluntary admissions to care, often short-term. Care orders are compulsory orders by the courts, committing children to public care.] Short-stay cases decreased slightly. It therefore appeared important to study such time-limited, change-oriented processes as could be evolved as an alternative to the relatively short approved school/ community home type of placement, rather than long-term substitute homes.

(3) Boarding out declined sharply, but it is the most individualized, the most flexible and the most economical form of care for all age groups.

(4) There is a constant shortage of residential places. Most of the evidence on the success of residential institutions for older children is negative, they are difficult to staff and enormously expensive.

(5) Supervision of children 'home on trial' increased sharply, and, hopefully, this is becoming a better understood and more effective way of helping. Family placement for treatment purposes would be seen as an extension of this approach – the placement using limited-term separation as a deliberately chosen means of concentrating on the resolution of difficulties.

After further discussion during the first few weeks of the project it was decided to make one important change to the initial guidelines: it was agreed that the age range of children to be placed should be narrowed to 14–17 years. There were two reasons for this decision. First, there was consensus among social workers that this was the most difficult age group to place; second, as the sample of cases dealt with by the project would inevitably be small, it was better to reduce the variables, where this was possible, by excluding pre-adolescent children.

It was decided that handicapped adolescents would not be included, as this would have increased the complexity of the project. In particular, schemes for 'normal' adolescents provide a bridge to adult independence, whereas severely handicapped young people may need a permanent sanctuary. This radically changes the task of the foster-parents. For this reason the following handicaps were excluded: severe physical disabilities; mental handicap – that is, handicap severe enough to prevent attendance at a school for the educationally subnormal (ESN); long-term mental illness.

Thus in its final form the project became one of a number of alternative forms of treatment for adolescents with problems. Obviously, the preferred treatment is to maintain the adolescent in his own home as far as possible or in a 'normal' environment, such as accommodation connected with institutions of further education. At the other extreme some adolescents, who may be more or less orphans, require a true substitute home. Intermediate treatment and the time-limited project placements lie between these two extremes. Table 1.1 shows the range of treatment available at

Table 1.1
Range of treatment available to adolescents with problems

Help at home (usually open-ended)	Home and away	Time-limited, task-centred treatment away from home	Open-ended treatment away from home	Open-ended substitute home or lodgings
Direct social work (a) casework with the adolescent	*Time-limited* Intermediate treatment	Placements for a limited period with professional foster parents, who would concentrate on the adolescent's perceived problems and difficulties, and remain in contact with his family	Available in a range of residential centres. Provides experience of group living, ranging between the extremes of:	Private family offering care and affection to adolescents without acute problems
(b) work with the whole family	*Open-ended* Part of the week in residence and part at home, boarding school, day care, etc.		(a) a relatively closed and structured environment including school and most other facilities on the premises	
(c) attendance at a therapeutic group				
(d) material or financial aid				
Indirect social work Improvements in the environment, e.g. school, leisure, work, etc.			(b) an open environment in which most decision-making is shared and school or work is outside	

the present time, including the project. Although these provisions exist in theory, their availability is very patchy. For example, few adolescents will have the opportunity of attendance at a therapeutic group.

A leaflet was printed for distribution to all existing foster-parents. It set out the available fostering careers as follows, making clear that any foster-parent could apply for any type of work.

Opportunities to offer care and help in your own home to children and young people

(1) *Day care* All or part of the day for pre-school children. Part of the day for those of school age.

(2) *Holiday homes* For children who attend boarding school. Must be regular commitment. Recognized scale of payments.

(3) *Short-term foster care* Family care for a limited period for children who are in need because of parental illness or other temporary difficulties. Recognized scale of payments.

(4) *Long-term foster care* Accepting a child as a member of your family for a long or indefinite period. The parents may or may not wish to visit but the child must understand the situation. Some placements lead on to legal adoption. Maintenance payments. Social worker visits regularly.

(5) *Foster care with additional responsibilities* (a) Family care for children with special difficulties or handicaps. (b) Foster care as rehabilitation – care of the child is combined with help to his family in order to facilitate his return home. Special allowance is paid. Social worker visits regularly.

(6) *Special family placements* Special help to older children and adolescents with particular problems of adjustment. Time-limited, problem-solving; not a substitute home. Professional fees are paid; membership of training and support group is expected.

THE HISTORICAL MOMENT

The project would never have started if the paths of certain key people – Nicolas Stacey, Vic George and myself – had not crossed at a particular moment.

Nicolas Stacey had been appointed Director of Kent County Council's Social Services Department late in 1973. He inherited a department which was far from problem-free after two previous changes of principal officer and the Seebohm reorganization. In addition, Kent had never had a high rate of fostering and had never developed an adequate network of small family group homes, and the buildings of the Poor Law children's homes were still in use. Furthermore, a community home with education for delinquent boys (Northdowns) was in considerable difficulties and was subsequently closed. The moment was therefore right for the development of a new and progressive strategy of child placement, and the new director persuaded the Social Services Committee and the staff of the department to embark on a radical programme designed to reduce residential care and to develop fostering and intermediate treatment.

At the same time I was employed as a lecturer in social work at the University of Kent and had just completed a comparative study of child placement in Sweden and Belgium. I had returned to Kent feeling highly critical of English placement policies, in particular the current clamour for more and more residential provision. Vic George had recently been appointed Professor of Social Work and Social Administration at the University of Kent. He had a long-standing interest in fostering, and through him the project received the academic support of the university.

Nicolas Stacey was quick to appreciate the possibility of importing European placement policies into an English Social Services Department, and he approached the Gatsby Charitable Foundation for funds to launch an experimental project. The Gatsby Fund supports promising new ideas which seem to be too risky for the investment of public money, and the Foundation generously agreed to pay the staff salaries for a five-year demonstration project. It certainly was a risk, as almost everyone assured me that I was attempting the impossible: 'It is bad enough living with one's own adolescent children; whoever would conceivably want extra ones?'

In a more general sense, the moment was right for an experiment of this kind. Donnison has described a social service as 'a continually developing response to continually changing needs and problems';[4] the Kent project was just such a response to the changing pattern of child placement.

THE DEVELOPMENT OF CHILD-PLACEMENT POLICY IN ENGLAND

The Children Act 1948 had marked the start of present-day child-care practice. The services for children which had fallen into disarray during the war were reorganized under newly appointed Children's Officers, one of whose first tasks was to modernize and split up the old Poor Law children's homes and to place as many children as possible in foster-homes in the community. The enthusiasm of the staff of these new departments is reflected in the national boarding-out rates, which rose from 35 per cent in 1949 to 44 per cent in 1954 and then to 52 per cent by 1963. However, disillusion followed as the placements made by inexperienced staff began to break down. Although no overall figures of breakdown were published, various studies showed that between 48 per cent and 59 per cent of long-term fosterings broke down. If all such studies are considered together, about half of the long-term placements led to breakdown.[5] There are very few studies of the quality of placements, but Rachel Jenkins's studies of a small sample of placements made between 1958 and 1961 suggest that a third were considered by social workers to be unsatisfactory.[6]

However, these sweeping generalizations disguise a number of important factors. There were wide local variations in practice, and early boarding out concentrated on young children with weak or non-existent parental links, a population among which many today would be considered eligible for adoption. Only a small proportion of the boys and girls who entered care at adolescence (generally only those who had no criminal record) were boarded out. In other words, fostering was for 'innocent victims' only.

Research into the breakdowns tended to concentrate on the children's previous experience or the qualities of the foster parents.[7] Only George describes fully the confusion of roles and relationships, the unprofessional level of social-work practice.[8]

Foster care was considered to be the provision of a substitute home for a long or short period. There was no job description or training for foster-parents, and the work was to be carried out purely for love of the child, money being paid for maintenance only. No research was undertaken into the significance of matching (the process of interaction whereby certain families may succeed with a particular child and fail with others or a child fails in one home and succeeds in a different one).

So the tide began to turn and residential care for children returned to favour. Of course, throughout this period residential care had never been *out* of favour for delinquent boys and 'beyond control' girls.The approved schools, prior to 1969, existed outside the Children's Departments and provided residential 'character training' and education for delinquents aged 10 to 18 years. They were the direct heirs of the reformatories but were influenced by the image of the public schools in which the children of the rich lived as boarders. When, following the Children and Young Persons Act 1969, the approved schools were made part of the general child-care systems and were renamed Community Homes with Education (CHES), the assumption that delinquent and 'beyond control' adolescents should be placed in residential institutions was never questioned. This assumption is reflected in the publications of the Department of Health and Social Security (DHSS). The only publication on foster-care is *Foster Care – A Guide to Practice*, which hardly mentions adolescents.[9] On the other hand, up to 1980 there were 21 publications concerning residential care, with a heavy emphasis on adolescents.

From about 1965 the proportion of children in foster care dropped by over 15 per cent, for several reasons. First, as has been mentioned, after the wave of enthusiasm for fostering that followed the Children Act 1948 there was a period of disillusion as placements made by the new Children's Departments broke down. This trend towards less fostering was reinforced by a reduction in the number of unwanted babies as a consequence of improved contraception and the availability of abortion, which caused the numbers in care aged 0–5 to drop substantially. At the same time the reorganization of the Social Services Departments to provide a generic service abolished specialist posts and sacrificed the old child-placement skills. Finally, after the 1969 Act delinquent adolescents were included in the statistics, which further reduced the proportion of children in foster-care.

However, if by the early 1970s the number of children under five entering care was declining, the number of older children received into care was rising sharply, the increase in care orders being particularly abrupt. Although prior to the Children Act 1948 local authorities had been *required* to board out children who were the subject of Fit Persons Orders, this requirement had been dropped in subsequent legislation, and a consensus had emerged that disturbed or delinquent adolescents were 'unsuitable for fostering'.

Thus boys and girls who entered care over the age of 14 years were not usually placed in foster-homes. For example, there were 890 boys and girls over 14 years of age in the care of Kent County Council's Social Services Department on 1 November 1975. Of these 480 were boys (40.9 per cent of all boys in care) and 410 were girls (45.0 per cent of all girls in care). (These are estimated figures based upon a 20 per cent survey of all children in care in Kent.) By far the greatest number of care orders were made for boys and girls aged 15. In Kent between 30 June 1976 and 30 September 1976 16 care orders were made for young persons of this age. The highest total for any other year of age was seven.

The 890 boys and girls were accommodated as follows:
(a) Numbers boarded out
     Boys 45 (9.4 per cent of all boys aged 14+)
     Girls 95 (23.2 per cent of all girls aged 14+)
     Total 140 (15.8 per cent of children aged 14+)

Number placed in foster homes after their fourteenth birthday

Boys 25 (5.3 per cent of all boys aged 14+)

Girls 50 (12.2 per cent of all girls aged 14+)

Total 75 (8.5 per cent of all children aged 14+)

(Of these, 20 boys and 35 girls entered care after their 14th birthday.)

(b) Numbers in residential care

Boys 205 (42.8 per cent of all boys aged 14+)

Girls 130 (31.8 per cent of all girls aged 14+)

Total 335 (37.7 per cent of all children aged 14+)

(c) Numbers placed under supervision at home

Boys 105 (21.9 per cent of all boys aged 14+)

Girls 135 (33.0 per cent of all girls aged 14+)

Total 240 (27.0 per cent of all children aged 14+)

(d) Numbers placed elsewhere, i.e. in residential special schools, detention centres, remand centres, Borstal, hospital, lodgings, residential employment and including long-term absconders. (There were some children from the Kent County Council in prison at the time of the survey but numbers were too few for them to appear in the sample.)

Boys 120 (25.0 per cent of all boys aged 14+)

Girls 55 (13.4 per cent of all girls aged 14+)

Total 175 (19.7 per cent of all children aged 14+)

The girls were thus seldom placed in foster-care after their fourteenth birthday and boys even more rarely. There may have been many reasons for this practice, such as the low rate of payment to foster-parents, but there was no evidence to show that adolescents do not enjoy and respond to normal family life.

Between 1950 and 1970 the Children's Departments had developed residential assessment centres, originally for a mixed age range. When the Children and Young Persons Act 1969 removed the distinction between deprived and delinquent children, assessment centres and remand homes were merged and, as a result of the changing ages of children in care, became full of older children and adolescents who were 'unsuitable for fostering'. This stagnant population had to be shifted into other residential institutions, and by the mid-1970s there was considerable clamour for the expansion of residential provision.

Thus the placement situation at that time was that a small proportion of adolescents returned home under supervision and benefited from the gradually developing Intermediate Treatment services; a few teenage boys and girls entered psychiatric units, in which the sexes tended to be mixed; but the majority were placed in residential establishments on the principle of like with like (disturbed girls with disturbed girls, young delinquent boys with young delinquent boys, older male offenders together and so on). Many did not go out to school or work, as education or occupation was provided on the premises.

BELIEFS OR KNOWLEDGE AS A BASIS FOR POLICY-MAKING?

All placement policies are shaped by beliefs rather than by knowledge. Some countries believe in residential care and do not use foster-homes. Others have reduced their institutional care to an absolute minimum. As we have seen, England has always had a roughly half-and-half pattern and believes in foster-care for young, normal children needing either short-term care or long-term substitute parents, but not for adolescents, particularly delinquent and disturbed ones. However, English placement policies have changed following changes in attitude. In the 1950s there was a belief in specialized services. Approved schools catered for one sex and one type of symptom (delinquency) and developed further to cater for younger, backward boys, older boys of different types, disturbed girls and so forth. It then became clear that a specialist system sent the adolescents to far-distant places, ignoring links with their homes and their local culture. Regional planning sought to ensure a greater degree of localization at the cost of less specialization. The next step was the merging of homes and approved schools in the wake of the Children and Young Persons Act 1969, which ended the administrative separation of offenders and deprived children.

However, the outcome of these changes does not seem to have been quite what was expected. Pat Cawson's national survey carried out for the DHSS in 1977 showed that the generation of children then under care orders was younger and less delinquent than the pre-1971 approved school generation.[10] Many were committed at their first court appearance, and most of them were placed in residential care immediately after the care order. Fostering was practically never considered. These children, mostly adolescents, often spent many months in assessment centres and then proceeded to community homes that offered education on the premises. While in residential care, the children's rate of offending was high. However, of those placed home-on-trial, rather fewer offended.

David Thorpe's work rounds off this picture.[11] It is true that it is the magistrates or judges who make the orders under which adolescents enter either penal establishments – Borstal, detention centres or remand centres – or other institutions catering for offenders, such as community homes with education on the premises. But by and large these orders follow the recommendation of the social workers, so that it is they who are the prime movers in committing adolescents to institutional care. Thorpe's study of offenders who were made the subject of care orders Basildon and Rochdale showed that 89 per cent did not require residential care, there being no reason why they should not live in the community. He also found that care orders were singularly ineffective as correctional measures regardless of placement and no more effective than any other measures in preventing crime.

Very gradually, in England Intermediate Treatment is beginning to develop ways of maintaining boys and girls in the community, but most troubled and troublesome adolescents are still admitted to residential care as a first resort, in spite of ever-increasing evidence that this form of care is both counter-productive and expensive. For example, Clarke's and Cornish's follow-up study of Kingswood boys compared two regimes, a conventional structured regime and a therapeutic community regime.[12] The re-conviction rates over three years for both regimes were 67 per cent for those released on after-care and 75 per cent if all releases are

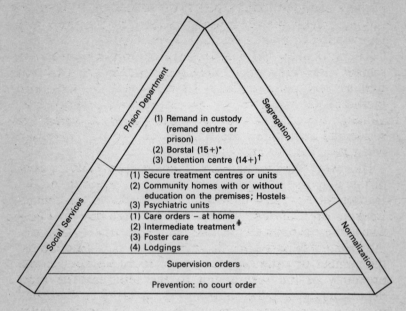

Figure 1.1
Provision for children and young persons
up to 18 years, 1975–80

* For boys and girls over 15 years of age. A sentence of 9–12 months is generally served, which includes some education or training. Of those referred to Borstal, two-thirds have been in community homes and half in detention centres. 25 per cent of the 15/16-year-olds have a history of absconding.

† For boys over 14 years of age only. Sentences are for 3–6 months, but with remission only 6 weeks may be served. Of those in detention centres, half have already been in institutions, and half have already been under a care order. A third have had no previous convictions.

A mixture of supervision at home, group activities and short periods away from home, organized and directed by a social worker. Set up by the Children and Young Persons Act 1969, it developed very slowly in the 1970s.

included. The authors suggest that 'only for about 20 per cent of those admitted to the school could it be argued that institutional intervention had provided more than a temporary interruption of their delinquent behaviour.'

The work of the Dartington Research Unit described some schools with good morale, offering enjoyable experiences, as well as very poor schools, but confirmed the long-term inefficacy of this form of treatment.[13] In other words, although some boys and girls had quite good experiences in residential care, there was virtually no transfer of benefits when they left the institution.

However, belief in the merits of institutions is carried even further in some of the debates on secure accommodation. The Dartington Research Unit brings the evidence together in *Locking Up Children*.[14] The selection of the boys and girls who at present enter secure units is largely a matter of chance, the strongest factors being the failure of previous placements, the number of letters written by the social worker and the proximity of the secure unit to the referrer. The most depressing factor is the outcome. About 25 per cent proceed to other closed institutions; of the rest, 75 per cent enter custody within two years. The financial cost of these units is astronomical. Cawson's and Mardell's DHSS study of the children referred to these units states that the tendency is to admit younger and younger juveniles to them.[15] It also states that such units fulfil a dangerous function in enabling normal community homes to reject difficult children:[16]

> The indications that some open units are unable or unwilling to cope with the normal problems of the child care system are as clear in this study as they were 18 years ago when the first units were planned. Now, as then, the clamour for more secure places may be used to divert attention from the need for general improvements in the child care system. . . . It is rather frightening that the capacity for rejection in the child-care system should seem so endless.

To complete a bleak picture, the re-conviction rate within two years for young people leaving Borstal was 85 per cent; for boys discharged from detention centres the rate was 75 per cent. Since 1968 the number of young offenders sent to penal institutions had increased faster than the rise in juvenile crime, and at the same time fewer supervision orders were being made.

With the exception of those boys and girls who were sentenced to detention centres or Borstal and went there from their own homes, adolescents requiring placement were generally committed by the courts to the care of the local authority Social Services Departments under care orders (compulsory measures which are operative until the young person reaches adult status at 18 years, or, if the care order is made rather late, until his or her nineteenth birthday). In other words, in England coercive measures appear to be considered essential in dealing with this group of young people, although this belief is not shared by all countries. In other respects also England differs quite sharply from other European countries. England and Wales have the lowest permissible age for criminal prosecution (ten years), with the exception of Scotland (eight years), in northern Europe. Corporal punishment is almost entirely banned in schools and children's homes in north-west Europe but is generally permitted in England and Wales.

So in the 1970s English practice was firmly wedded to compulsory residential care for the majority of adolescents whom the courts were reluctant to allow to remain in their own homes. On the whole, the principle of placing like with like was followed. These practices were sustained in the face of mounting evidence that this very costly system of residential care was counter-productive.

Against such a backcloth, there seemed little danger in initiating an experiment to foster adolescents. It could hardly do worse; and if one justification for undertaking such an experiment was that the existing policies for adolescents were ineffectual and expensive, another was that elsewhere other approaches seemed to be distinctly more hopeful.

PLACEMENT POLICIES IN BELGIUM, SWEDEN AND THE UNITED STATES

In 1971 the theme of the annual group research sponsored by the Social Committee of the Council of Europe was 'social measures regarding the placing of children in community homes or foster-families'.[17] The researchers (from Malta, Austria, Sweden and the United Kingdom) studied the 17 countries of the Council of Europe.

Any report with such a broad theme and which relies on very different legal systems and methods of collecting statistics must inevitably be superficial, but the general picture that emerged was clear enough. In some countries three-quarters of the children and adolescents in the care of public and voluntary bodies lived in foster-homes. In other countries foster-care was not used at all. The determinants of these differences did not appear to be wealth, population or geographical factors, but rather beliefs about what was best. The total volume of research on this subject was extremely small. In fact, the only careful comparison of groups of children in their own homes, with foster-parents and in institutions was a small study carried out by Duhrssen, in Germany, in 1958.[18]

As the United Kingdom member of the team, I became extremely interested in these differences, and, with the financial help of the British Academy, I carried out a small, independent study of the use of fostering and residential care in Sweden, Belgium and the United Kingdom. Sweden represented a high fostering country; Belgium relies on residential care; and the United Kingdom has always had a half-and-half pattern. The data was collected in 1974.

Belgium

In Belgium children were received into care either by the courts and committees responsible to the Ministry of Justice or by the local Poor Law authorities. At the time of the Council of Europe Study 12 per cent of the children in the care of the Ministry of Justice were boarded out. The Ministry was eager to promote this form of care, and by 1974 the figure had risen to 16 per cent. The complete figures for the Poor Law children who were placed by the communes (small local units) were impossible to obtain but were probably similar. Normally, only children without severe difficulties who needed a substitute home were placed. Belgium has a long-standing suspicion of foster-homes on the grounds that it is difficult to monitor what happens in small, scattered families. On the other hand, Belgium is a Catholic country and collects large sums from church congregations for children in need, which are used to build and maintain institutions. The state relies heavily on residential care provided mainly by denominational voluntary bodies and often run by religious orders, and although there are some small homes in Belgium, very large institutions are still being built. The rationale is twofold: it is easier to ensure good standards if all the children are in one place; and as the care of deprived, disturbed or delinquent children is held to be a matter for experts, it is easier to provide a range of experts in a large institution.

Thus the contribution of lay people in their own homes is devalued, and it is considered appropriate to provide children with treatment by psychiatrists, psychologists, teachers, speech therapists, remedial gymnasts, social workers, pediatricians and so on. The experts pool their findings at frequent case conferences. This is an enormously expensive system. Its benefits are unsupported by research findings, and it stands in stark contrast to Sweden's 'whole person' approach; but change will be difficult to achieve because of the formidable vested interests with a stake in the *status quo*. The situation in the United Kingdom is in some ways comparable, with the trade unions and the Residential Care Association taking the place of the Church and the Union of Voluntary Organizations in Belgium.

Sweden

In Sweden the Royal Commission on the placement of children and young people published its report in 1974. There is practically no provision by voluntary organizations or agencies for child care in Sweden, and there was, at that time, a specialist public child-care service. The report stated that 70 per cent of children in public care up to the age of 15 lived in foster-homes and that this method of care was satisfactory. Only 10 per cent of the children exhibited severe difficulties. The research was based on factual data and the opinions of foster-parents and social workers. The families of origin and the children were not consulted.

At that time the number of children's homes and the occupancy rate of the existing homes were declining.[19]

Where adolescents were concerned, a substantial number lived in foster-homes or other small, private arrangements of various kinds. There were few facilities that could possibly be described as 'residential care', and those that there were generally had many vacant places. The most delinquent adolescents and those hardest to control were admitted to the national youth welfare schools. These schools had a 'revolving door' policy, so that boys and girls were placed with families as soon as possible, with the possibility of recall to the institution. In 1974 more inmates were living outside than inside. (On the day I visited a school for 100 boys only 14 boys were actually living there.)

Thus in 1974 about three-quarters of the boys and girls under 18 years of age were in public care in the community, but there is one very important factor which distinguishes the situation in the early 1970s from the early 1980s. A high proportion of the foster-children under 15 years of age studied by the Commission were single, illegitimate children, placed in long-term substitute homes a long way from their area of origin. In 1980 single parenthood is no longer stigmatized, and the housing, financial and other support available to one-parent families means that a single mother can now keep her child if she wishes. In addition, modern contraception and abortion have prevented the birth of many unwanted children. In other words, the population of children needing long-term substitute homes has almost ceased to exist, a fact which is likely to reduce the number of children in foster-care.

The Commission recommended fostering as a method of care but pressed for the acceptance of four principles: *normalization* – the right to live a normal life in the community, making use of the normal community resources for education, health care, employment and so on; *localization* – the right to remain in one's home area and not to be sent away; *voluntariness* – the right to choose (coercive measures are only acceptable as a last resort); *participation* – the right to take part in decision-making.

Since 1974 Sweden has methodically developed these four

principles by changes in the law and in practice. Social-work departments are now generic, and where children are concerned, the main thrust of their work is to improve family functioning so that the children need not be removed and to reduce reliance on coercive measures. An Act was passed by the Swedish Parliament in 1980 which was designed to reduce compulsory powers over children. It stated that if a compulsory order is made because of the incapacity of the parents, it must be reassessed and, if appropriate, renewed annually. If a child or young person is compulsorily removed from home because of his own behaviour, the order must be reconsidered every six months, otherwise he returns home. It has been Swedish practice to look upon one year as the maximum period that any child should spend in residential care. The law already states that once a child has been in residential care for six months, he must be reported to the Government board (Social-styrelsen) every three months, and reasons must be given for his stay.

The youth welfare schools are changing into mixed communities for various client groups with localized catchment areas, and the 'treatment' concept of youth prisons (similar to Borstals) has been abolished, all youths now serving a determinate sentence in the same way as adults. However, incarceration is used only for extremely persistent or dangerous offenders.

The Swedish belief is in the 'whole person' approach where the client is helped through a relationship with a social worker to use the normal resources of the community, or where he is helped by lay people acting as foster-parents or by befriending families (support families). Residential care is either a very temporary affair or a last resort. Nevertheless, although present Swedish policies place even more emphasis on maintenance in the community, the actual number of children in foster-care is likely to decline as a result of the changes which have been described.

The findings of the Commission so far discussed relate to *all* foster-children, but in 1974 Sweden had also developed fostering for the care of children with special needs. For very disturbed children special rates were paid, and foster-parents were expected to work closely with child guidance clinics and schools. For adolescents small-group foster-homes for four or five boys and girls had been developed, with quite a generous rate of payment. Even the most difficult adolescents were successfully placed in private families, as Kålveston describes in her excellent study of 40 foster-families.[20] At the same time the Stockholm child-care service had experimented with family placements in the north of the country for big-city adolescent drug addicts. About 30 per cent of the placements appeared to be successful – a very high rate for this particularly difficult group. However, the distances and difficulties involved meant that this system of placement failed to develop in the long run.

It was clear from the Swedish experiences that even the most difficult adolescents, including delinquents, could be maintained in foster-care, and that the role of residential care could be drastically reduced, with generally positive results. In particular, allowing more delinquents to remain in the community (fostering by youth welfare schools and other schemes) did not seem to affect the overall rate of offending.

The fact that the maintenance of delinquent and disturbed youths in the community does not increase the crime rate or produce any dramatic public response has also been demonstrated in the United States, where developments in Massachusetts have confirmed the Swedish findings. In other words, the success of these policies does not appear to be determined by specific cultural or geographical factors. However, the process of change in Massachusetts has been very different from that in Sweden.

The United States: the Massachusetts experiment

If in Sweden residential care for children and young persons faded away as a result of general agreement on the principles of placement and the deliberate development of policy along these lines, residential establishments for young offenders in Massachusetts were closed abruptly in a situation of conflict.

In 1969 Massachusetts had a system of large, rurally isolated institutions for the custody and treatment of young offenders that were similar to those in many European countries but often harsher than the English approved schools. The institutions were the target of considerable public criticism.

In 1969 Dr Jerome Miller was appointed the first Commissioner of the newly constituted Department of Youth Services. He sought energetically to humanize the institutions, obtaining considerable help from the media. Young people were encouraged to speak of their own experiences in order to illustrate the havoc inflicted by institutions on the lives of juveniles. However, staff resistance and vested interests held up progress to the extent that by the end of 1971 Miller was certain that decarceration was not going to be successful, although the population of the schools had been reduced. The final step in 1972 was therefore the abrupt closure of all institutions, followed by a confused but creative period in which a wide range of alternatives was developed.[21]

The Department created a wide variety of programmes by buying facilities from the voluntary sector or by contracting with new or established agencies. For example, young people (not necessarily those with professional qualifications), were encouraged to plan creatively for the needs of youth in trouble. Secure institutions were not abolished totally, but the number of young offenders who could be placed in secure settings was limited by establishing a low-capacity ceiling.

In 1970 a major study of the events in Massachusetts was undertaken at the Centre for Criminal Justice at the Harvard Law School, under the direction of Professor Lloyd Ohlin. The reform had given rise both to high expectations and to prophecies of doom, but the Harvard evaluation showed that neither recidivism rates nor costs differed significantly from the previous system. (The costs of the Massachusetts institutional regime were probably lower than the English institutional costs for the same age group, as Massachusetts relied more on large, regimented institutions.) Nevertheless, this statement hid certain realities. Recidivism had not increased in spite of the rising age of the delinquents and the increase in delinquency rates nationally. The general public was not terrified by the presence of large numbers of extra delinquents in the community. On the other hand, the institutional setting had produced more negative subcultures and had effectively isolated the young people from the community compared to the community-based system.

Professor Ohlin has summed up the situation as follows:[22]

> It is our opinion that the community-based system is a workable alternative to a training-school system; at least as effective as the institutional system, no more expensive and far more humane. The changeover in Massachusetts demonstrates that the vast majority of delinquents can be handled in relatively non-institutional settings. However, our research indicates that *the network of relationships which youth maintain in the community have a crucial impact on their ability to stay out of trouble on their release.* In fact, it seems clear that the total community experience of the youth before and after his correctional experience may overwhelm even the most constructive elements of the correctional programme. The development of constructive ties with family, schools, work, church, recreation, etc., are a necessary follow-up to the programme. Supportive social contacts established during a youth's enrolment in the community-based correctional programme must be provided after his separation from the programme if the gains made during the programme are to be maintained. (Italics are mine.)

There is a very strong argument for localization and normalization in placement. The English system of residential care breaks these community linkages but does not offer anything in their place. Fostering should achieve a better transfer of learning after placement because either it does not break the links or it establishes new ones.

SIMULTANEOUS EXPERIMENTS IN FAMILY PLACEMENT

Europe

At the time that the Kent project was being planned initiatives had been taken almost simultaneously in a number of countries to develop family placements for older children and for adolescents with severe problems. It seemed as if the tide was beginning to turn; the old stereotype of substitute homes was being challenged by new methods.

In 1974, when the project was being prepared, information about these experiments in paid foster-care was gradually becoming available. In that year in West Germany Bonhoeffer and Widemann published a collection of papers on foster-care.[23] They described experiments in working with hard-to-place children and young persons in Groningen in the Netherlands, in Sweden and in Bremen and Kassel in West Germany. At this time similar experiments had also begun in Berlin and in Denmark (and probably in other places too – social workers often fail to record and publish their best innovative work).

The project run by the welfare authority of the German province of Hessen was of particular importance to Kent. I was able to visit the scheme in 1978, and their published evaluation was a mine of information (see Chapter 6).[24] By 1978 the Hessen project had placed over 200 older children and adolescents and was pleased with the results. The children were placed with families who, with a few exceptions, included one member with an appropriate qualification (in psychology, child care and so on), and a professional fee was paid. Support was provided by the project workers and by fortnightly meetings with expert consultants. A vivid picture of the start of a placement, written by one of the foster-parents, has been translated into English.[25]

It is somewhat surprising that no experiment of this kind appeared at that time to have been undertaken in France, where there is a long tradition of fostering, which has been written into the law as the first choice of placement for children in care.

The United States and Canada

During the period since 1974 a substantial number of schemes similar to the Kent project has developed in the United States and Canada.[26] Possibly the best-documented of all schemes was the Alberta Parent Counsellors Project, which placed children aged between 12 and 16 years.[27] This scheme operated as a research project from 1974 to 1977 and has now become a part of Alberta Social Services.

From its experiences the Alberta project suggests that

using the public media is the best way to recruit foster-families and to interpret the programme to the community; it also claims publicity of this kind generates a large enough pool of applicants to permit the selection of suitable families. (In this project selection was unavoidable, as the number of places was limited.) The project recommends that appeals should be realistic rather than emotional, stressing first the job and then the income, training and support components of the programme. It is also important for applicants to receive a prompt response.

The project developed a training programme of orientation meetings, pre-placement meetings and fortnightly meetings during the placement. (Some social workers felt that the families were not critical enough of each other in the groups, and they were reluctant to work with natural families.) The criterion for the selection of children to be placed was the severity of their problems. Those who were persistently delinquent, violent and aggressive or were frequent ab-sconders were particularly carefully considered and did, in fact, prove most difficult in placement.

The Alberta project defines the foster-parents' role as that of the primary worker. The social worker acts in an advisory and supportive capacity to the Parent Counsellors and has little direct contact with the child or natural family. This approach stresses the need for all participants to work as a team, using group methods, in order to achieve specified goals. A detailed plan is agreed at the start and reviewed every two months, the Parent Counsellors taking responsibility for writing regular progress reports.

Some children are able to return home after a period with a Parent Counsellor family; others may need an extension of placement or may be moved to a more permanent foster-home. Some older children stay in the family supported by student grants or earnings; others remain as ordinary foster-children. Decisions about such issues are difficult ones, which can only be solved on an individual basis.

The Professional Association of Treatment Homes (PATH), Minnesota, is particularly interesting, as it was developed in 1972 by a group of foster-parents who were dissatisfied with their experiences in large, seemingly insensitive agencies.[28]

PATH parents are defined as staff members of the agency and, as such, are expected to be actively involved in planning their own in-service training programmes as well as in the development of agency policies and procedures. All foster-parents receive 24 hours of pre-service training and are required to attend two evening staff meetings per month. All placements start with a very carefully negotiated contract.

PATH, as an agency, is under the full control of the PATH parents. The board consists of PATH parents who are accountable to their units. PATH parents are responsible for interviewing and selecting their own psychological consultant and the social worker who will provide them with services. The usual relationship between foster-parents and social worker has been reversed therefore; in this case the social worker is clearly accountable to the PATH parent.

The United Kingdom

In 1975 the care provided for the majority of adolescents in the United Kingdom was residential; lodgings or foster-homes were available for a minority of those with less acute problems. Professional fostering with defined objectives and high pay was practically unknown.

However, one local authority, Reading, which sub-sequently became part of Berkshire, had a professional fostering scheme which was already operating in 1974. Under the leadership of Mary Hartnoll, this scheme placed older children with severe difficulties with salaried foster-parents. These families were considered to be staff members and attended staff meetings at the divisional offices. Some training was provided. There were both successes and failures in the first phase of about a dozen placements.

Certain disadvantages of a salaried scheme soon became clear. If a family does not in practice turn out to be very successful, it still has security of job tenure for many years – but how can it be used? No selection committee can ever hope to predict future success accurately. In addition, families change. A happy marriage may fail, or illness may radically change the balance of forces in the family, so that the home becomes inappropriate for fostering. On the other hand, this scheme gave security and pension rights to the families, which they are denied under a fee-earning scheme. In subsequent years Berkshire developed a mixed pattern of salaried and fee-earning families. It is interesting to note that the Kent families have never shown any interest in transferring to a salaried status.

CONCLUSION

The projects outlined above have been based on high payment for a 'professional' service and appear to have shown encouraging results. However, both traditional fostering, which provides the child with a substitute home and for which payment is related to costs rather than profit, and adoption, whereby parental rights are permanently transferred and no payment is made, have recently begun to extend their activities to include more older and handicapped children and to develop new methods of work.

Kadushin[29] has reported on the successful outcome of adoptions of older children, and Donley[30] has described the work of the Spaulding Organization in arranging for the adoption of older and handicapped children. In the United Kingdom several voluntary organizations have started to develop these methods, with promising results. Their work is described in Triseliotis's review of new developments in foster-care and adoption.[31] Local authority Social Services Departments are also breaking new ground in this way.

2 Questions of Theory and Method

THEORY

In the past fostering was always considered to be the provision of a substitute home for children unable to remain with their own parents. Early fostering was rather like adoption; social workers made little attempt to link foster-parents with the parents of origin. Gradually, social workers began to place more emphasis on working with the family as a whole in order to prevent reception into care; thus the natural parents became much more important. The work of Rosamund Thorpe showed how often the natural parents had been ignored and how it was possible to work more closely with them.[1] Holman's definition of 'inclusive' and 'exclusive' fostering clearly formulated the dilemma but did not develop fully the concept of a partnership between foster-parents and the natural family.[2] In practice, the natural families were seldom more than visitors to the foster-home – sometimes welcomed, more often resented. The idea of a foster-family as a *complement* to a natural family remained embryonic – and, of course, because so few adolescents were boarded out their special needs were seldom mentioned.

If the foster-home was a substitute family, the foster-parents were deemed to be 'in place of parents', and fostering has been based on the concept of *parental* relationships. Almost all writing concerned with foster-care has been based on psychoanalytical assumptions, taking into account traumas caused by early changes of caretaker and the transfer of a child's insecurity and anger into the new situation. Much has been written about a child's difficulties in coming to terms with more than one set of parents and about the stresses of discontinuity in the socialization process. All this has been helpful in enabling social workers to respond more sensitively to the needs of young children. This traditional approach to the finding of substitute homes for young children is faithfully reflected in the DHSS publication *Foster Care – A Guide to Practice*.[3] It seems as if the fieldworker's heart is with young children, but adolescents, with their high nuisance value, belong to the residential sector.

Further, although early fostering was regarded as simple home-finding, more recent developments have seen placement as a step towards restoring a child to his parents, a change that has given foster-parents the extremely demanding task of loving a child and integrating him into their family in order to make him strong enough to return to his own (often very stressful) home. How dangerous this can be if the child's voice is not fully heard is shown by the report of the inquiry into the death of Maria Colwell.[4] However, the needs of adolescents are not the same as those of younger children. Although it is assumed that they will go home, 17 or 18 years old is not the age to return to Mummy and Daddy; it is the natural time to leave the nest.

Finally, for young children in placement emotional difficulties can cause problems in foster-care – unresponsiveness, lying, stealing, soiling – for which a 'cure by love' is appropriate. Adolescents, however, come into direct conflict with the law, and society insists that their behaviour should be controlled.

Because of the almost total absence of theory about the foster-care of adolescents, the project felt that it was important, from the outset, to make an explicit statement about the theoretical basis of its work and the social-work methods to be used. It is interesting that this blueprint has stood the test of time and that no changes have been made during the five years of the project. As Donald Winnicott used to say, 'There is nothing so practical as a good theory.'

The attempt at a theoretical synthesis
If little has been written about the foster-care of adolescents, an enormous amount has been written about their deviant

behaviour, and there is no consensus about causes or remedies.

The motivation to initiate the project sprang in part from the considerable volume of sociological writing which shows that deviance is largely socially defined and that the process of labelling an adolescent as delinquent or disturbed may serve to launch him into a deviant career rather than to check the process. Similarly, the removal of deviants to institutions – like-with-like placements or ghettoes – may well socialize them into, rather than out of, deviance.

The debate continues over whether delinquents should be considered unsocialized individuals or calculating transgressors of the legal order. The Children and Young Persons Act 1969 enshrines both concepts: the full machinery of .courtroom adjudication is retained for those who see delinquents as responsible; an emphasis on social welfare exists for those who see them as the 'non-responsible' product of social circumstances. Traditionally, social workers have traced the roots of delinquency to the family – to poor relationships with parents, broken homes, absent fathers and poverty – but in so doing have tended to undermine the individual's responsibility for his own behaviour. The whole apparatus of 'treatment' rests on the 'diagnosis' of what is wrong and the application of a remedy. The paternalistic overtones of this attitude cannot be missed: adults know best what is good for adolescents, and in particular the advice of qualified social workers and other experts should be followed.

Adolescents in public care do indeed generally have severe family difficulties, but the project is not persuaded that their future is determined by 'family pathology'. In fact, the Dartington research team found that while adolescents in approved schools, and particularly those in secure units, did have very disturbed (family) backgrounds, they were not *as* disturbed as the families of other children in care.[5] In other words, institutionalization is not a function of family disturbance. The project believes that present difficulties must be tackled, and the adolescent may need help in doing this (help, for example, in seeing his parents realistically), but this does not equate with the medical model of 'treatment'.

The interactionist perspective, on the other hand, does not seek to explain delinquency by attempting to identify differences between delinquents and non-delinquents. It reserves the question 'Why do these adolescents commit offences?' and instead asks, 'Why is it that there are adolescents who do not commit offences?' The answer appears to be that virtually all adolescents and adults commit offences but some develop a commitment to delinquent activity (or other forms of socially unacceptable or self-destructive behaviour) and a reputation which effectively ensures that infractious behaviour is seen as the most important characteristic of that person. These are the clients of the project, and the *commitment to delinquent (or otherwise deviant) activity* is the key to the whole operation.

The fact that behaviour is the product of interaction between individual and environment explains why adolescents behave in different ways in different situations – they may be polite and conformist at school but disobedient and rude at home, violent in a large institution but gentle in a small group and so on. The danger is that a derogatory label will stick and will influence subsequent responses. (For these reasons the project has always been sceptical of assessment because it almost always takes place either in an unhappy home or in the artificial environment of residential care.) The interactionist model offers hope of change by altering the environment. In Mischel's words:

> whereas in accord with trait theory it had been assumed that an individual's position . . . would be relatively stable across testing situations and over lengthy time periods if the test instrument was sufficiently stable . . . voluminous research in the last decade repeatedly shows that performances . . . can be modified by a variety of stimulus conditions, and provide little support for the existence of stable, broad, unchangeable personality traits.[6]

However, if the environment is changed, the adolescent must be capable of modifying his behaviour in response to this alteration. The project has always accepted the importance of learning theory, particularly the principle that behaviour that is rewarding will be repeated and, conversely, that change may be feared because of previous bad experiences. Obviously, happiness in placement is the best possible reinforcement.

Learning theory, however, does not seem fully to account for the turmoil which is often, but not always, a feature of adolescence. The project considers that adolescence is a time of change, a developmental crisis in the transition from child to adult. Because it is a time of change, physically, emotionally and socially, it is a time when the adolescent can choose and follow new directions and when outside influences can be brought to bear on these choices.

The project found Erikson's concept of identity formation to be a satisfactory theoretical basis.[7] Erikson believes that adolescents go through a period of identity crisis or a turning-point over an extended period of time, which may involve considerable stress and instability, especially if previous childhood conflicts remain to be resolved. But adolescence is also viewed by Erikson as a psychosocial moratorium, a period when decision about adult identity and role may be delayed and role experimentation indulged in. It is a time for exploring and testing the possibilities for one's future and more binding adult identity without having to make any firm commitment.

Adolescence is characterized by the conflict between identity and identity confusion and the need for fidelity, someone or something to be true to. The resolution of the identity crisis marks the end of adolescence and the beginning of the first adult crisis (intimacy versus isolation), so that this identity, formed and consolidated during adolescence, constitutes the core of the adult personality.

Sullivan has emphasized that adolescence is the period when puberty adds sexual desire to the need to achieve interpersonal intimacy; often lack of competence in interpersonal relationships, especially those with the opposite sex, creates difficulties for attempting to form integrated relationships in which the primary needs for security and intimacy are met.[8]

Erikson's view is that identity must be *achieved*:

For identity is not simply given by the society in which the adolescent lives; in many cases, and in varying degrees, he must make his own unique synthesis of the often incompatible models, identifications and ideals offered by society. The more incompatible the components from which the sense of identity must be built and the more uncertain the future for which one attempts to achieve identity, the more difficult the task becomes.[9]

For every adolescent in care the formation of his own synthesis is a particularly difficult task, in which he requires adult help. But the maturation of his own cognitive processes should provide him with some of the tools he needs for the job. Piaget has shown how at adolescence cognitive development moves towards the capacity for abstract thought: 'No longer exclusively preoccupied with the sober business of trying to stabilize and organize just what comes directly to the senses, the adolescent has, through this new orientation, the potentiality of imagining all that might be there.'[10] Thus the adolescent, much more than the child, moves through the realm of the hypothetical. The basic orientation toward the real and the possible leads him naturally toward formulating and testing hypotheses about his environment. For the adolescents in the project, learning to think their way through their problems was always seen as an objective of placement.

Finally, thinking oneself into a new identity involves moral choices. Garbarino and Bronfenbrenner have suggested that this highest level of moral autonomy will only be achieved

in a setting in which an individual is provided with opportunities, security and social support for the development of abstract thinking and speculation as a product of partially competing and overlapping social allegiances . . . a setting in which there are competing social loyalties, dissonant enough to promote a measure of tension, but not so incompatible as to be overwhelming . . . orientation to principle rather than control by social agents is predicted upon a social structure characterized by multiple social agents to whom the child is attached and who are 'pulling' him in somewhat different directions.[11]

This evidence seems to support placement in a foster-family in which security and social support is provided; the dissonance between the family of origin and the foster-family provides competing and overlapping social allegiances; the structure and ideology of the project supports individual choice and autonomy rather than following group norms (as in residential care).

So, in theoretical terms, the project considered that its objective was to help adolescents to sort out their present problems. Adolescents were seen as ordinary human beings in a situation of particular difficulty. Most of them had had negative experiences in their past environment and had failed to develop positive ways of dealing with problems. However, it was considered that they could not avoid taking responsibility for their own lives and must work their way through the normal crisis of adolescence to form a viable adult identity.

Placement in a new situation produces a jolt of discontinuity, shaking old assumptions and posing new questions. This can help the adolescent to use his developing cognitive powers to explore new possibilities and to experiment in a new field of action. A foster-family does not provide him with substitute parents but with helpful adults who will encourage him to talk about and work out his problems for himself and will give him appropriate practical help and information. In this situation differences of social class and lifestyle between the foster-family and the family of origin are significant only in so far as they provide sufficient discontinuity but not too much.

Group living in residential care does not provide the same opportunities for two main reasons. First, it is difficult to continue the crucial dialogue when staff change, either because of shifts and holidays or because of resignations. Second, where staff attention is divided between group members, no one staff person can act as the individual champion and helper of one adolescent. In foster-care the adolescent has one or two people completely on his side – generally a new experience for him, as most boys and girls have never before been carefully and consistently listened to and supported. Although the adolescent may wish to speak of his past in order to explain the present, work is clearly focused on problems and opportunities here and now. He may be helped to develop a new and friendlier relationship with his own parents but is under no pressure to return to their care as, at 17 or 18 years of age, his developmental task is to establish himself as a young adult, capable of loving and working.

METHOD

The project's decision to focus on problem-solving in the present as a step towards building a new life in the future meant that the methods used would inevitably differ from the casework approach of traditional child care.

The foster-parents' role

It was decided that the foster-parents should play the central role. They would be expected to work hard and would be well-paid. One placement was considered the equivalent of a part-time job; two placements was regarded as one person's full-time employment. (The payment was in two parts, a taxable professional fee and the normal tax-free boarding-out allowance which only covered the costs of the placement).

The foster-parents were seen as colleagues, equal in esteem and status to social workers. They were expected to assume responsibility for implementing the treatment plan that had been established at the inception of the placement and to work with the family of origin. The project echoed exactly the role definitions made by the Alberta Project:[12]

> In summary, the role description, functions and expectations that were planned for parent counsellors were significantly different than for foster-parents. Their preparation included specially designed recruitment, selection, and training experiences: their primary function was the management of all services for the child and family in their care; and their accountability rested with clients, agency, and their parent counsellor colleagues. In short, they were to be given responsibility commensurate with the capabilities that we believed they possessed, and they were to be provided with appropriate support, recognition, and financial remuneration. . . .

We began, too, with a firm conviction that natural parents must be involved in the planning, goal setting, and service activities that would be characteristic of our programme. We assumed that natural parents would commit themselves to be involved in desired change activities and that parent counsellors would aid in this process through frequent communication and resource acquisition where appropriate. We did not subscribe to the notion of a social worker managing or restricting communication between the two sets of parents, as there seemed to be persuasive evidence from other programmes that such caution was both unnecessary and unworkable.

Thus we began with a good deal of optimism that natural families could be involved productively in our service plans, and that while the specifics of this involvement would need later explication, we hoped our service model would lead to better results in this respect than are typically reported in foster care.

One of the cornerstones of the Kent project was the belief that lay people, in their own homes, can carry out many of the tasks professionally assigned to experts and that they will not generally need the social worker to act as intermediary or go-between (see Figure 2.1).

If the role of foster-parents is increased, the 'expert dominance' of the social worker is correspondingly reduced. The project felt that there was very little knowledge on which to base either the selection of foster-parents for 'treatment' placements of adolescents or the 'treatment' methods to be used. Rather than being vetted by social workers, foster-parents would therefore enter the scheme by means of an educative process which would enable them to find out for themselves whether they wished, and felt confident enough to embark on work of this kind. Such methods, based on groups, had previously been employed to recruit adopters in the United States.[13]

The enhanced status of the foster-parents also meant that they would share in the overall development of the project on equal terms with the professionals, although final decisions concerning resources obviously remained with the Director and Social Services Committee.

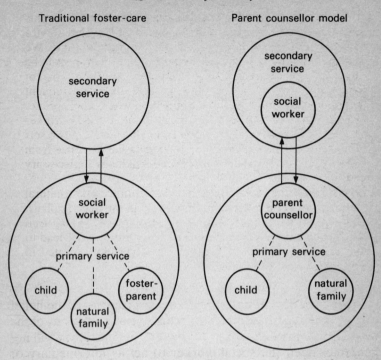

Figure 2.1
Administrative responsibilities

Tasks and time-limits

The project planned to follow Reid's and Epstein's model of task-centred casework.[14] Reid's and Shyne's work in the United States on time-limited contracts had shown encouraging results, and this had been further developed into what Reid and Epstein call a 'formal system of intervention'.[15] Task-centred work makes two essential value assumptions: first, that the client's expressed and specific understanding of his problem is accepted without recourse to explanations of his troubles in terms of unconscious needs and so on; second, that reliance is placed as far as possible on empirically tested theory rather than 'practice wisdom' or untested theory. In this method work starts with the social worker and client collaborating in a search to define the problems, which may then be ranked in order of importance. The next step is to work out the tasks which will be the means of reducing or solving the problems. At each stage the client must understand and agree to the plan.

The project accepted two fundamental principles. First, placements would be time-limited rather than open-ended, as evidence appeared to show that time limits force focus and selective attention on the part of both social worker and client. They also appear to hold anxiety in check by keeping to the point: 'What I can do *now*?' Second, placements would have explicit problem-solving objectives. Adolescents should understand the purpose of a placement and must agree to it.

These two principles were combined in the use of contracts, which set out the objectives of the placement and the agreed areas of work.

Contracts

Contracts were central to the project's concept of 'treatment' placements, providing both an agreed statement of objectives for all concerned (adolescent, family of origin, foster-family and social workers) and at the same time providing the foster-parents with a job description – which had been notoriously lacking in traditional fostering.

Since the appearance of Reid's and Epstein's work on task-centred casework, contracts have been used in both field and residential settings, with variable success. In some instances the difficulties relate to a failure to agree on definitions. For example, in his study of a very good approved school/community home for delinquent boys Walter demonstrates the staff's professed desire to 'help' the boys with their 'problems' (defined by the staff as family problems).[16] The boys, on the other hand, saw their objective as getting out as soon as possible and considered that good behaviour was the best way of achieving this. Walter concludes: 'thus the general orientation of the boys militates against their perceiving themselves to have the sort of problems indicated by the official philosophy.' This means that the basis for a contract (agreement on the problems to be tackled) is missing.

In other instances contracts have not been reciprocal.

Contracts have been used in some Borstals, but in such cases the 'contract' appears to have been entirely one-sided, the boy undertaking to carry out certain specified activities or to abstain from others, while the staff and social workers are not bound by any kind of reciprocal agreement.

The principles underlying the Kent contracts were clarity and reciprocity. (George's research describes how social workers have failed to define the roles and tasks in conventional foster-care.)[17] The contracts therefore sought to define the time limits and objectives of the placement and to ensure that all participants (the adolescent, the natural parents, the foster-parents, the divisional social worker and the project worker) agreed about the definitions. When the match was first proposed the aims and time limits were discussed informally before any introduction was made. Once the adolescent had visited the foster-home and had decided that he would like to remain there, a contract meeting was called at which all participants assisted in drawing up the formal agreements. Obviously, these agreements had no force in law, but they were formal statements of intent.

There were four separate agreements. The contracts for the adolescent and the foster-family were almost identical – the adolescent undertook to do certain things and the family undertook to help him to do them. The contracts for the divisional social worker and the project worker divided the administrative and social work tasks between them. Until the last year of the project there were no written agreements for the family of origin, although as far as possible they participated in working out the other contracts and generally agreed to certain tasks or arrangements. Jerry Roberts was the first project worker to begin to develop contracts that included the natural parents, an example of which is given below.

The contracts generally followed the same outline. The first paragraph set out the estimated length of the placement, the requirement for a six-monthly review and the procedures to be followed if the placement were terminated earlier. No party to the agreement could terminate the placement without giving four weeks' notice, unless everyone had agreed to an alternative plan. In fact, the divisional social worker was legally empowered to remove the adolescent at any time, but it was highly unlikely that such a drastic step would be needed, except when the adolescent had to be admitted to a hospital or other safe place without advance warning or when he was arrested. The rule that four weeks' notice must be given and that the foster parents shared the responsibility for planning the next step certainly prevented 'spur-of-the-moment' breakdowns.

The second part of the contract listed the objectives under four headings: the undertaking to live as a family member; arrangements relating to the family of origin; intentions concerning school, work or other occupation; specific problems to be worked on.

*Contract for the placement of Jean Smith
with Mr and Mrs Graham and family*

The placement will be from the 16th September 1979 for six months in the first instance. It will be reviewed at the end of six months to see if any changes are needed and may be extended at the end of the first period. The placement may be ended at any time if all concerned have agreed on an alternative plan, otherwise one month's notice must be given, during which time every effort must be made to arrange a constructive transfer.

The aims of the placement are:

FOR JEAN
(1) To live with Jim and Elizabeth Graham as a member of the family, adjusting to the family rules or guidelines and giving a fair hearing to advice and guidance from them.
(2) To keep in touch with her own family so that she can work towards understanding their feelings and wishes and to keep in weekly contact with mother.
(3) To continue attending her present school and to work hard towards gaining good qualifications for a career in the WRAC.

FOR JIM AND ELIZABETH
(1) To accept Jean into their home and help her to live as a member of the family, giving a fair hearing to her point of view and to arrive at a compromise when necessary.

(2) To encourage her to maintain contact with her family.
(3) To encourage her to do well at school and assist her in preparing for a career.
(4) To meet monthly with the divisional social worker and Caroline (Jean's mother) to discuss progress.
(5) To try to understand Caroline's position and to express their feelings to her in a frank and open way.
(6) To attend project family groups and prepare quarterly reports relating to Jean.

FOR CAROLINE
(1) To try to understand Jim and Elizabeth's position and to express her feelings to them in a frank and open way.
(2) To keep in weekly touch with Jean and to work towards understanding her feelings and wishes.
(3) To maintain her interest in Jean's education and career.
(4) To keep in contact with the Divisional social worker and Jim and Elizabeth, meeting monthly to discuss progress.

The experience of the project seemed to indicate that it was better to draw up quite short, simple contracts and to amend them fairly frequently at reviews. Nothing was included in the contract which the adolescent did not recognize as important, and it was crucial not to set the objectives too high. The adolescent kept a copy of his contract and took pride in ticking off the 'problems' that he had tackled successfully. If the adolescent was bound by this statement of intent to live in a certain way and to work on certain problems, the foster-family was bound to help him and could be questioned about how it set about the task.

The contracts for the project worker and the divisional social worker were also generally drawn up along standard lines.

Contract for the Project Social Worker

(1) The project worker will be responsible for the payment of the professional fee.
(2) The project worker will be responsible for the support and professional development of the foster-parents. This will be carried out by visits to the foster-home and through the group meetings.

(3) The project worker is responsible for ensuring that the objectives of the placement are understood by the foster-parents, implemented or modified, and that the outcome is defined and evaluated.

(4) The project worker is responsible for ensuring that the adolescent understands the objectives and plans and for ensuring that his/her co-operation is enlisted.

(5) The project worker is responsible for ensuring that the initial contract is drawn up and reviewed at six-monthly intervals or more often if appropriate.

(6) Copies of all project records will be sent to the division.

Contract for the Divisional Social Worker

(1) To arrange for the payment of the normal boarding-out allowance, the initial clothing grant and any other payments which may be agreed under the normal regulations for boarded-out children.

(2) To maintain contact with the adolescent's family of origin, ensuring that they understand the purpose of the placement, to undertake any social work with them which is considered necessary, and to inform the project of any changes which take place.

(3) To visit the adolescent in the foster-home. These visits will have two purposes:

    (a)   to help the adolescent to come to terms with the reality of his/her family situation and to make sure that appropriate links are maintained between the family members.

    (b)   as the legally accountable person, to ensure that this placement is good enough, in view of the adolescent's particular needs. To maintain or establish a relationship of trust and friendship with the adolescent, so that he/she has an outside person in whom he/she can confide or to whom he/she can complain if he/she wishes to do so. It is anticipated that the divisional social worker's visits will not be fewer than the minimum requirement of the boarding-out regulations, unless a special arrangement has been agreed for the project worker to act on the division's behalf.

(4) Copies of all relevant records will be sent to the project.

It is particularly important that the divisional s̶ ̶ ̶ ̶ worker should develop a relationship of trust with ̶ ̶ adolescent, as he is the one powerful outsider to wh̶ ̶ ̶ ̶ ̶ ̶ he boy or girl can complain. (The project worker m̶ ̶ ̶ ̶ too closely identified with the foster parents' poi̶ ̶ ̶ view). He is also legally accountable for the qua̶ ̶ ̶ ̶ ̶ ̶ the placement.

As is evident from the specimen contracts, both project and divisional social workers were obliged to send each other copies of all records, and, of course, it was important that they should consult over all decisions. It was also felt that the contracts for the social workers should go beyond a simple division of labour and should be linked more specifically to the contract aims specified for the adolescent, foster-parents and parents of origin. Thus not only would the social-work tasks be defined, but the contract would also convey to all concerned that these agreements were reciprocal, in that *all* parties were accountable to each other in working towards achieving their aims.

The project workers and foster parents were agreed about the usefulness of contracts. A contract helps a family to see more clearly what is expected of it, and it helps an adolescent both to focus on certain areas in which he can achieve visible progress and to gain experience in negotiating and keeping agreements – a very important social skill. It gives him some sense of being in charge of his own life, rather than being the passive recipient of decisions which have been reached by adults in his absence.

When the project started it was intended to follow the Reid and Epstein method more closely than proved possible in practice. The project contract set out the aims quite satisfactorily, but it was intended to develop a second stage of specified tasks to be undertaken in order to achieve those aims. This was abandoned, first because the situation was so complex that it was difficult to decide which tasks to select, and, more important, because it was essential to leave the foster-parents free to work spontaneously in their own style – to be true to themselves.

Reviews
The boarding-out regulations require that foster placements

should be reviewed, and this requirement was included in the contracts. The first review should normally be held three months after placement. However, during the first few weeks of a project placement negotiations took place, culminating in a meeting of all concerned, at which the contracts were drawn up. It was obviously pointless to hold a review meeting close on the heels of a contract meeting. For this reason the first review was often simply an administrative operation, whose purpose was to check that everyone had received a contract, that a medical examination had been arranged and so on.

The review which is officially required every six months was an entirely different matter, however. These reviews were held either in the project office or in the foster-home. Ideally, those present should have included the adolescent, his natural parents, his foster-parents, the project worker, the divisional social worker (usually accompanied by the principal social worker) and any other person with an important contribution to make, either 'outsiders', such as teachers, or 'insiders', such as natural or foster-siblings. No review could be held in the absence of the adolescent, foster-parents, project worker and a divisional representative, but it was inevitable that natural parents would not always attend, for various reasons. Some lived a very long way away or had disappeared altogether; more frequently, both parents had remarried, and there was considerable stress within the family. Occasionally, the parents had totally rejected the adolescent and refused all contact. It was only in most exceptional circumstances that they were not invited, however.

The review meeting generally dealt with the issues which the division wished to raise, based on their standard review form, and it also considered the adolescent's progress in relation to his project contract. Amendments to the contract could be made, and it was encouraging if the adolescent could tick off certain 'problems' as dealt with and set himself new goals.

Reviews were considered extremely important. The meetings were formal and in no sense designed to rubber-stamp existing placements. Adolescents did not always like such formal meetings but they could be helped to express themselves and to acquire self-confidence and a sense of the importance of the issues which were discussed. Such meetings made the implicit statement that the future of the young person was worth very serious consideration.

Recording

When the project was set up it was made clear that the families would be expected to keep records of their work. At first it was agreed that a diary should be kept and entries made at least weekly. A full report was to be provided for the six-monthly review. However, the diaries constantly lapsed and were, for long placements, distinctly tedious, so it was agreed that the families should write a quarterly report and use diaries only to help them as an *aide-mémoire*. Families were also expected to provide reports for court hearings. Occasionally, adolescents were willing and able to write reports on themselves.

Report by Nick Jones (aged 15) on his placement with Mr and Mrs Watts
I am free to do as I please in the house that is reasonable and I think that I am trusted. I am allowed to come and go as I wish as long as I let Iris or Ben know where I am going and what time I will be back if I know myself. They are very tolerant with me because, for example, they said I could have a dog on the condition that I behaved at school. I didn't, but still they let me keep the dog.

I think that Pat and Billie treat me as one of the family. They appreciate me as a babysitter because I do not shout at them. If they don't do as I ask them, I just leave it, because they usually do as I ask them to anyway. When Jill [the divisional social worker] was here last week, I said that Ben goes up to the pub when Iris was at work sometimes, thinking that it didn't matter whether he did nor not. When Jill had gone, Iris expressed her annoyance about it, and when she mentioned it to Ben, he in his turn was annoyed. As a result, they won't go out at all, which makes me feel guilty about it because I didn't mean to say I meant that Ben went every night.

They took me to Spain with them which was greatly appreciated by me. We all enjoyed ourselves in Spain; we all got on well together apart from a few ups and downs. I also appreciated the trip to the Edinburgh Tattoo which I think Iris and Ben paid for and which was organized by a friend of hers, who I went with. I have been going to guitar lessons once a week which Iris has been paying for out of her own money. They also bought half of the guitar, with Social Services, for me for Christmas which I am glad of. It was suggested that I went out more, but I have found this a little difficult to do on my present pocket money. For example, it costs 44p one way to Maidstone and about the same to Chatham, so I would have hardly any money when I got there, and it would take three weeks' pocket money to go to the pictures. I have made quite a few efforts to get a part-time job but nothing comes of it and only last week I sent off details for a part-time job.

In conclusion, I must say I couldn't have wished for a better home than this and I appreciate all they do for me.

Report by Iris Watts on Nick Jones
Nick now is happier than we have ever seen him, having just returned from what appeared to be a successful two-week holiday with his family and no real prospect of school in sight to dull his spirits – he appears to have achieved his aim, having told the Headmistress of the Retreat Centre that he had no intention of going back to school and would misbehave to ensure his permanent suspension. Despite the jobs around the house we found for him to do during school hours, with the usual breaks for coffee, lunch, etc., he remains cheerful, friendly and co-operative. He is a great asset and I should be pleased, but inside I cry for him. We have tried to make him understand how bad it is for him to be at home, but we cannot get through to him. He likes being a housewife. If he were a girl (apart from the schooling), he would be admired for his efforts. He only complains when he is asked to do a more vigorous or manual job, like window cleaning or gardening. When he starts work, he will not, in our opinion, be capable of holding any labouring job.

Ben believes that we have not been at all successful with Nick since he was suspended. He feels Nick should be sent to a boarding school and given no more 'chances' – for his own good. Only with the help of David and Jill [the project worker and divisional social worker] were we able to point out the progress we had made, persuade him to change his mind and expect less. I can see his view point very well; he put it very strongly at the last review meeting. His relationship with Nick remains unchanged. There has been no loss of respect for him by Nick.

As far as friends are concerned, Nick remains alone – girls come calling for him from time to time, but nothing materializes. The nearest he gets to friendship is with our two younger boys. They both like Nick and he is fond of them.

Most important for Nick was his recent visit home. He says his mother wants him back again. He gives me the impression that she is worried that he may transfer his affections from her to me and this could perhaps explain her wanting him home on a permanent basis or not at all attitude. Her fears are unfounded as Nick loves and needs her very much. Her monthly visits ceased approximately four months ago. We made an attempt to send Nick for odd days, but this also appeared to upset her.

Last Christmas [1978] Nick felt he had been neglected by his family regarding Christmas presents, so we waited this year until he came back to us before giving him anything; we wanted to avoid him receiving too much or too little in proportion to his own family and our own children. I think this time Nick is to be believed when he told me again the difference in proportion between his present and his young brother's. It did not, however, deter him from enjoying his holiday with his family. I hope we can regard this as progress. We have tried to explain to him that life isn't always fair, but the more you put into it, the more you get out of it. Coping with the injustice he feels (not only at Christmas time) and whether justified or not, would perhaps help him when he finally returns to his family.

The use of groups

Groups of foster-parents, working together, were seen as the keystone of the scheme. From its inception the project relied heavily on the concept of people helping each other. This is a model which anyone can understand and which can be used for almost any age and kind of person. In this situation the role of the social worker is that of convenor and enabler. The project made no attempt to develop any models of therapeutic group work, which would place the social worker in a very different role, analogous to the one-up relationship of doctor–patient.

From the start it was intended that the foster-parents should meet regularly to help and support each other and that the project social worker should attend these meetings. The meetings would be work sessions rather than social gatherings, with the focus on describing and evaluating the work being done. Meetings would enable the families to get to know and trust each other, to feel less isolated, to help each other in times of difficulty and to share their skills. There was no intention of imposing any set pattern on individual groups, and there were many precedents of successful self-help groups (families of handicapped children, disabled adults and so on).

A further purpose of group meetings was to develop a sense of corporate identity. In 1975 the fostering of adolescents with severe problems was considered an impossible task, and at that time institutions were the automatic form of placement. Through comparison of paid fostering with the known shortcomings of the large institutions, a group ideology in favour of decarceration was created. It was also obvious that the groups would provide training for the task to be undertaken. No attempt was made to work out a specific syllabus in advance, in order to avoid the kind of education which Freire describes as 'banking' – that is, a system in which the teacher has the role of 'narrator', presenting a reality to be learned as if it were motionless, static, compartmentalized and predictable.[18] It was hoped that each group would develop its own training, and that both teachers and students would co-operate in 'unveiling reality'.

Finally, it was hoped that the groups would be the instrument of the selection of project families. There did not appear to be any reason to believe that the fairly meagre research findings indicating which families would be most likely to provide successful substitute homes for young children would be valid for time-limited placements for adolescents. The co-operative group mode of operating on the one hand and, on the other, the lack of any reliable method of predicting future success in this new form of fostering seemed to indicate that the project worker could *not* undertake to pick out which applicant families were acceptable.

Fortunately, there were precedents in other ways of working. In the United States Kirk had developed new methods of selecting adopters.[19] He rejected the formal vetting procedures, even eliminating written checks on such matters as health and police convictions. All applicants joined a group in which a joint decision was gradually reached about whether or not they should proceed to adoption. (The application of the 'educative' method of selection is described very well by Hagen, following experience in the Adoption Unit, Lutheran Social Service of Minnesota.)[20] The project did not accept the elimination of official inquiries, such as health and police checks, but felt that it was in keeping with the equalitarian ideology of the project and with the general lack of knowledge to offer applicants the opportunity of discovering for themselves, by attendance at group meetings, whether this was the kind of work they really wanted to do and whether they had the necessary aptitude and facility for it.

Self-selection was limited by the social worker's role as matchmaker, however. The project worker received information about the adolescents to be placed and knew the families who wanted a placement. Obviously, he would not suggest that a particular adolescent might be suitable for a certain family unless he believed that the placement would stand a chance of succeeding. This limitation meant that some families who needed a special age or type of boy or girl might have to wait for a placement. But the situation would be clearly explained at the group.

The placement families were organized in groups (according to locality) for fortnightly meetings. Normally, the minimum size of a group was five families; when over ten families had joined the group usually divided. On 1 August 1979 there were seven regular groups and one occasional group consisting of five scattered families.

After an initial interview at their home, applicants were invited to attend a group. The aim was to help them to decide, with the guidance of the other group members, whether this kind of work was what they wanted to do and, if so, to develop in them a commitment to the ideas of the scheme and to prepare them for placement. Regular attendance of both

parents at meetings over a period was a prerequisite   r
placement, as well as continuing attendance as far as poss.
during the placement, although it was sometimes difficult i
both parents to attend all the time once a teenager was place
in their family. The meetings gave the project staff an
opportunity to get to know the applicant families in a more
natural way than at formal interviews and to decide whether
or when a placement would be made with them. Mainly,
however, the process of entry to the scheme was one of
self-selection. Entrants to the group either progressed to the
point of placement or decided to leave, and the group helped
them to reach their decision.

Pre-placement meetings tended to discuss the problems
of adolescents and the attitudes of the couples to them,
child-care policy and practice and related issues; and occasionally groups invited experts (juvenile court magistrates
or psychiatrists, for example) to the meetings. Most
groups were held at a residential establishment situated
at a point in the county which was convenient for five to six
couples to reach. The role of the project worker in the group
was, first, to organize the meetings (to ensure that the room
was available, that everyone knew the date of the meeting
and so on) and to keep a brief record. Second, his task was to
enable the group to perform its agreed functions. In practice,
this role was rather like that of a referee. He had to ensure
that everyone did not speak at once and that tasks were
defined and carried out. He could make suggestions but could
be out-voted.

The groups varied in character according to membership,
and, once they had acquired their own identity, two functions
seemed to be particularly important. First, they provided
mutual support in relation to particular or general problems
with placements. (This included taking in each other's
children in periods of difficulty.) They also tended to create
an informal social network, and people met outside the
groups, particularly those living close to each other. The
children (foster and natural) of the project families were
invited to attend occasional meetings, and in this way all the
local participants got to know each other in an informal way
and the adolescents who were placed learned to understand

hat the project as a whole was trying to do. Second, the groups developed and criticized the policies of the project. They discussed such matters as the contracts, methods of evaluation and scales of payment and made recommendations to the Advisory Committee which, if it was in agreement, ensured that the recommendations were forwarded to the appropriate authorities for implementation. (The Advisory Committee, which generally met quarterly, was composed of foster-parent representatives of the groups, the project organizer and senior representatives of the department.)

Apart from the unsettling effect of changes in membership, which naturally tended to diminish the cohesiveness of a group, problems sometimes arose when the group seemed to try to perform more than one of its functions at the same time; for example, a sociable atmosphere could thwart a meaningful discussion, and particularly large groups tended to break into subgroups. Generally, the groups took their task seriously and invested considerable effort in working effectively as a whole without the necessity for very much leadership or intervention from the project staff. However, all groups went through occasional bad patches, when the project worker was required to play a more active role.

It had originally been hoped that basing the groups on residential establishments would place those establishments in a central position, like the hubs of wheels, from which outposts (foster-homes) would radiate to form local networks. It was hoped that the establishments would perform the vital functions of supporting and training the families and generally servicing the scheme (by helping with readmission in moments of crisis and in other ways). Although the project encountered unstinting good will on the part of residential staff, the original concept was not fully implemented. The main reason for this failure was the scattered nature of the referrals and placements in a small project working in a large county. In addition, not all appropriately sited homes had a room to spare for group meetings, so that other arrangements had to be made.

From the start it had been a problem to devise ways of involving the divisional social workers in the groups. Each group of families worked with adolescents from variou divisions, and each adolescent had a divisional social worker. The groups always met in the late evening for the convenience of the foster-fathers, but this was hard on social workers. At first, individual social workers were invited one by one, but this only served to exacerbate their sense of exclusion. The most satisfactory solution appeared to be for each group to hold regular 'open evenings' for divisional social workers, and these were generally well-attended.

As the groups developed, they became more self-confident and more effective in helping each other at times of crisis or stress, so that families seldom needed to be 'rescued' by social workers. On the other hand, the training aspect of the groups' work became more difficult. In the first phase, when all the families were inexperienced, it was quite easy to devise a programme of training and preparation for placement. In the second phase the groups consisted of experienced families and a trickle of newcomers. Although the experienced families were willing to help the newcomers, they did not want to keep recapitulating themes they had dealt with, and the process of preparation became distinctly haphazard.

Plans were made to remedy this in two ways. First, 'study days' were held at intervals on Saturdays. The 'study day' was attended by all recently recruited families and a number of experienced families. They followed a successful format devised at the first meeting. In the morning one lecture described the organization of the Social Services Department and a second lecture outlined the juvenile justice system. After lunch the participants divided into groups to discuss the work of the project. Second, a training subcommittee was set up, consisting of project families and social workers, whose task was to build up a cassette library. It was intended that applicants should take the tapes home, listen to them together and come back to the group with questions and comments. The tapes were to cover the history of the project, its aims and procedures, the effects on families of working with the project, child development (mainly adolescence), the structure of the social services, reception into care and the law in relation to adolescents, the education system, assessment of adolescents and so on. Tapes were to be made by project and departmental social workers, educationists and other appropriate people. However, by the end of the experimental period the cassette library had hardly started.

The groups were of immense importance to the foster-parents and project workers. From time to time the adolescents and older children of the foster-families were invited to attend, but they considered this a boring activity. The boys and girls in placement were also asked if they would like to have their own group, but there was strong resistance to this idea. They do not like being brought together and reminded of their status in care, and although individual friendships developed, there were such wide variations in age and ability that a local group would have had difficulty in developing a common purpose.

The project also considered the possibility of setting up groups for the parents of origin but did not proceed because of the practical difficulties. A great many of the parents of origin are divorced or separated, so that many adolescents have four 'parents' and numerous siblings. The families of origin do not always live in the same district as the foster-families, and many of them do not have a car. It appeared that the amount of work which would have been required to set up these groups was disproportionate to the possible benefits.

The network

As the project families came together in regular group meetings they developed a relationship with the project worker and also with each other, thus forming a network of social bonds. In addition, the various groups throughout the county kept in touch through 'study days', general meetings and occasional parties, so that an extended network also developed.

In this way a kind of 'artificial tribe' was created. Anthropological studies have described primitive societies in which children are valued highly and are welcome in every house in the village. In this situation, or where there is a close-knit extended family, children can take refuge with other welcoming adults in times of stress at home. Close-knit, localized extended families are now rare in European industrialized societies, and small nuclear families often keep themselves to themselves. It was felt that the network of project families could provide not only support and help among adults but also, for the adolescents in placement, the possibility of an easy transfer from one family to another 'within the tribe' when an existing placement was no longer wholly appropriate. Such a transfer would not be a leap into the unknown.

The creation of an 'artificial tribe' had affinities with the 'network therapy' of Speck and Attineave,[21] who rely on calling together all the friends and relatives (a process they call 'retribalization') in order to find a way of helping a family in difficulties. Their method, like that of the project, is based on the principle that it is better for people to help each other than to expect a 'cure' to result from the ministrations of the expert in charge, whether doctor, therapist or social worker. It did not seem realistic to expect a new foster-family's own friends and relatives to rally round to help, but the other foster-families were able to take their place or to supplement their efforts.

3 The Project in Action: Families, Adolescents and Placements

Between May 1975 and the end of July 1979 the project placed 156 adolescents, of whom 85 were boys and 71 girls. In mid-1979 about 57 families were working for the project in seven groups and almost 70 boys and girls were in foster-care on any one day. This chapter will consider how the adolescents were placed by the project, the characteristics of the boys and girls, the foster-families with whom they were placed and their families of origin.

THE PLACEMENTS

Referrals
The policy of the project was to accept any referral which fulfilled the two criteria of age (14–17) and severity of problem. An application form was completed by the divisional social worker and sent to the project together with any relevant documents, such as court reports, psychiatric opinions and educational data. If the application was in accordance with the project's criteria, the name was placed on a list, and the project workers then attempted to place the adolescents according to the order in which they were referred. However, this practice was subject to two considerable restraints.

First, after a slow start due to initial mistrust, referrals poured in, so that it was necessary to close the list for considerable periods in order to avoid a totally unrealistic waiting list. Second, placement was subject to considerations of matching, in that families could only accept either a boy or a girl of a certain age and with certain types of problem. The requirements of the available foster-homes did not necessarily correspond to those of the adolescent at the head of the list. Because queueing up for placement often took a long time, a number of adolescents who were referred found other destinations.

During the period from the end of March 1975 to the beginning of August 1979, 328 referrals were accepted. Because the list was often closed for months at a time, the numbers referred do not reflect the number of adolescents for whom placements would have been requested if the project had been larger. In February 1976 there were 2605 children in the care of Kent, of whom 42.7 per cent fell within the 14+ age range. Of the estimated 890 over 14s, 375 were offenders, 120 were non-offenders with histories of anti-social behaviour, 200 were children with histories of predominantly neurotic problems and 190 were children without histories of any major difficulty. Only 5 per cent of the boys and 12 per cent of the girls were placed in foster-care, so that the number of potential applicants for project placements was very high. (Figures have been estimated on the basis of a 20 per cent survey of children in care in Kent.)

Although the composition of the referral list was largely a matter of chance, it had certain interesting features. The number of boys and girls was equal for those of compulsory school age (106). This appears to reflect the fact that although there are generally more boys than girls of this age in care, girls with severe problems tend to be considered more difficult to place, but at the same time more suitable for family placements than wild and aggressive youths. The referrals tended to taper off towards the top end of the age range (69 boys and 47 girls between 16 and 18), which is not surprising as social workers are likely to consider that a very short placement would not be worth trying. Apart from the smaller numbers of older boys and girls, the ages were fairly evenly spread. Although the project workers were always convinced that there was a 'bulge' of 16-year-old boys, this does not appear to have been the case, but this group tended to take longer to place.

It seems possible to classify the referrals under a number of headings.

Preventive referrals:
This group was composed of adolescents with whom the divisional social worker was in contact, who were living in their own homes but for whom supervision or intermediate treatment facilities were inadequate or inappropriate resources. Either their parents had requested their removal from home, or the court was likely to make a care order. A carefully matched placement direct from home, without recourse to residential care, may work very well.

'Last chance' referrals:
These were boys or girls faced with the prospect of prolonged residence in either a penal or a psychiatric establishment. Family placement would be for them the last opportunity to live a normal life. The court was likely to agree to a deferred sentence in these circumstances, and the results seemed promising.

'End of the line' referrals:
These were the adolescents for whom the division, after trying everything it could think of without success, asked the project to help.

Institutional rejects:
This group comprised the adolescents who had been turned out of institutions either because they were too violent, too withdrawn or too delinquent etc, or because they were too old, for example, at school-leaving age.

The project never refused to try to place; a refusal to accept 'bad' referrals would only have penalized the adolescent in any case.

Matching
The referral form for the adolescents detailed their problems and their interests; the project families' form listed their assets. How did we set about matching the adolescents with these families so that the assets could be used to the best advantage to reduce the problems? In adoption and 'substitute-home' fostering there has usually been some attempt at

matching the child and the foster-home by criteria such as social class or intelligence, and the placement of children close in age to those of the natural family tends to be avoided (following Parker).[1] The criteria for matching within the project were somewhat different.

Age and personality:
The first proposal for any new match was reached through discussion at a meeting of the project team. Obviously, the personalities of the foster-family and the adolescent were carefully considered, together with their ages, general lifestyle and so on. How a match was made is not easy to explain. Sometimes a positive choice was reached by a flash of insight; at other times the process was rather to eliminate all the alternatives but one. (The analysis of the foster-families later in this chapter shows that couples of almost any age appear to be able to undertake this work, and very different personalities can be successful.)

Intelligence:
Treatment in foster-care requires a great deal of careful thought, and intelligence is an important criterion, but like-with-like matching was not considered essential. For example, intelligent families seemed to enjoy the task of rehabilitating retarded or handicapped adolescents.

Social class:
Again, we did not match for social class on a like-with-like basis. The more or less middle-class project families were perceived by us – and by the families of origin, of whatever social class – as professionals who offered a service. This did not dispose of all the difficulties related to educational and financial inequality, but it did make a working relationship possible.

Location:
In some instances the project families lived in the adolescent's home area, which facilitated the preservation and improvement of existing relationships. Sometimes, particularly in the case of delinquents, distance is an advantage, as it may help to break delinquent associations and may enable the adolescent to start his life again without the handicap of a bad reputation.

A certain distance also helps to cool off hostile family relationships. However, no placement was made more than a couple of miles outside the boundaries of Kent.

Place in the foster-family system:
We tried to work out as carefully as possible how the insertion of a new member would affect all members of the family. The children of any family are particularly vulnerable and, we were aware that we must not damage 'their' children by trying to help 'our' children. Usually a placement benefited the children of a family by enlarging their understanding if they were old enough to become aware of social problems, or by providing them with extra attention if they were very small. Time-limited treatment placements of adolescents differed from 'substitute-home' placements of younger children, in that companionship with others of the same age range was a great help rather than a danger. There was no pretence that the adolescent was a natural child of the family, and this seemed to reduce jealousy and rivalry, while the presence of children who were already integrated into the community helped the newcomer to find his place in local peer-group activities. However, if the children of the family turned against the newcomer, this was extremely difficult to deal with and could cause a placement to fail.

In the majority of cases placement meant a move to a very different environment. For children of one-parent families it presented the problem of relating to two parents; and for many adolescents the move was one from an urban, working-class environment to a more middle-class, rural style of life. The adolescents did not appear to find this transition difficult, and on the whole their parents considered that well-educated people with spacious homes could offer their children a professional service which could be respected and appreciated.

Symptoms
'Symptom' is a misleading term, and is used here merely to indicate the overt behaviour which made these adolescents eligible for the project.

Delinquency:
A total of 88 delinquent boys and girls were referred to the
project. Of these, 57 boys had convictions for theft, traffic
offences and assault. Some had an extremely large number of
convictions, and there were a few very serious offences. The
31 girls fell into two categories: the first included 17 girls who
had committed offences similar to the boys', though fewer
traffic offences and no indecent assaults; the second group (14
girls, labelled 'beyond control') had shown very unacceptable
behaviour – running away, sexual promiscuity, drinking and
so on – but had no criminal convictions.

Psychiatric disorders, maladjustment, emotional disturbance:
A total of 37 'disturbed' adolescents (9 boys and 25 girls) were
referred to the project. In addition, for two boys and one girl
low intelligence, rather than emotional disturbance, was the
main problem, in conjunction with very unfavourable social
circumstances.

Casualties of the system:
These were 21 adolescents (14 boys and 7 girls) who had spent
many years in care, in either one large institution, or a series
of residential centres, or a sequence of residential and foster
placements. They were attached to no one and had no roots
anywhere.

Other:
For five adolescents – one boy and four girls – the difficulties
lay in the extremely difficult problems which they had to
confront (for example, the consequences of incest or of a
particularly distressing form of hereditary disease) rather
than in their own behaviour. Three other girls, who did not
have particularly severe emotional problems, had become
pregnant at 14 years of age and did not want to give up their
babies. They also had to confront very serious problems.

Legal status in care
Boys and girls may be received into care for one of three
reasons. First, they may be subject to a care order under the
Children and Young Persons Act 1969. This order is made by
the juvenile court and invests the local authority with parental

rights and powers until the adolescent reaches the age of 18 years or, if the care order is made rather late, 19 years. This is a compulsory order and usually follows behaviour that is delinquent or 'beyond control'. Second, they may enter care under Section 1 of the Children Act 1948. This is a voluntary arrangement with the local authority, entered into by parents who are 'prevented' from caring for their children. The parents are free to remove their children from care at any time, although, as a result of the Children Act 1975, a period of notice has been made obligatory for medium and long-term placements. Third, if the parents of Section 1 children are dead, have disappeared or are deemed permanently incapable of caring for their children, or if the child has been in continuous care for three years, the local authority may assume full parental rights under Section 2 of the Children Act 1948.

In 1975 Kent County Council Social Services Department carried out a survey on a 20 per cent sample of children in care, which showed that in the 14+age group 73 per cent of the boys and 63 per cent of the girls were subject to care orders. The majority of boys and girls in the project had been the subjects of care orders. The numbers are shown in table 3.1. The Section 1 adolescents were often very disturbed or maladjusted and were particularly difficult to place. The project team was not at all sure that compulsory care orders were necessary for such a high proportion of the boys and girls. On the other hand, the Section 2 resolutions were virtually all a necessary response to non-existent or potentially very dangerous home situations.

Table 3.1
Project boys and girls under care orders, 1975–79

	Boys	Girls	Total
Care orders	66	37	103
Section 1	16	23	39
Section 2	3	11	14
Total	85	71	156

Corporal punishment

Corporal punishment was never considered acceptable within the project. Nevertheless, adolescents were occasionally hit by foster-parents (and vice versa). These incidents were generally discussed in the groups, and the project workers always made it clear that they would never support foster-parents who had hit a boy or girl if a complaint was subsequently made.

Corporal punishment for boys is permitted in all secondary schools in Kent. The project felt that it would not have been helpful to ask for the project boys to be treated differently from those living in their own families, and several of them were punished in this way. They did not like corporal punishment, but it was difficult to discern any subsequent effect on their behaviour. Improvement generally followed the change from loathing school to enjoying it – usually because of the achievement of some success or because of improved relationships with staff or peers.

Multiple placements

When the project was set up it was anticipated that the placements would be one by one (except for siblings placed together), in contrast to the like-with-like placements in residential care.

Before the end of the first year we had begun to add a second placement in a number of families, but we discovered that this was an extremely difficult operation, and we made a number of mistakes, either upsetting the original placement or failing to establish the second one.[2] However, in the long run we learned that a second placement could provide much-needed companionship and that the two could help each other.

We drifted into making three placements by accident. In the first case we had planned to place two friends together, but an elder brother insisted on being included, and this threesome worked very well. In another family we allowed a third placement to be added where one placement was almost completed and a second was well-established. In 1979 we agreed to a fourth placement in a family whose own children were by then grown up. However, we saw this as the point where group care begins and the one-by-one concept of fostering ends. After the second placement only a half-fee was paid.

In the view of the project team, far too many siblings are separated on the grounds that they do not get on together; too little effort is generally devoted to developing and improving inter-sibling relationships by increasing contact. To have a family network is sometimes even more important in adult life than it was in childhood. However, placement together was sometimes impossible to achieve, and even contact was often difficult to maintain. The project placed one pair of sisters and two pairs of brothers together, and the following siblings separately: two sisters from two families; three sisters from one family; three brothers from one family; a brother and a sister from one family. These siblings did not always show much interest in one another, but placement within the project system meant that they never lost all contact.

Foster-parents' salaries
The project sought to recruit a new population of foster-parents with the knowledge, experience and personal qualities needed to confront the most difficult teenage problems. It was crucial that the professional fee should be sufficiently high to compete with alternative sources of income, such as part-time teaching. (It is also a fact that in Britain more and more families rely on two breadwinners in order to maintain their chosen standard of living, to pay their mortgage and so on.) Money also makes life easier. While the addition of an adolescent to the household may cause considerable stress, there are real compensations if the family can afford to run a car, buy a new washing machine or have a really good holiday. Such realities make difficulties less insuperable. Finally, money confers status. It is a statement that the work is valued in the same way that the work of the professionals is valued. It also puts the families under an obligation to provide a reliable and efficient service.

The project adolescents knew that payments were made. Obviously, they did not like being paid for. ('Traditional' foster-children also dislike the idea that they are paid for.) This seemed to be a problem that could only be faced honestly and resolved by the foster-parents demonstrating that they worked not 'for love' but 'with love'. One of them put it this way:

> We would not undertake this type of fostering unless we were paid a reasonable salary – so we do not do it *for* love, but we do it *with* love.
>
> The fact that I am paid for my professional skills enables me to put up with disruptions and inconveniences that might otherwise cause strain and fury. I am often up in the early hours dealing with enuresis, and again at 6.15 a.m. to get her up for work – but this is the sort of thing I am paid for, and because I am properly rewarded, I do not need to reject the child who interferes with my sleep.
>
> Because she is not my own child, any tantrums and rudeness are not actually to do with me, and (unlike those of my own children) they are not caused by my faulty upbringing; therefore I am able to cope firmly but calmly, and although I may become angry, the anger does not linger and there is no crippling guilt.
>
> If the children complain that I listen to our girl too much, I can explain that it is my *job* and that I am not paid for nothing. This they understand, and also appreciate the extras they are now able to enjoy. It is hard work; it carries great responsibility, but we all enjoy doing it and are rewarded in many ways – if anything, I think we are a stronger family and more understanding people than we were a year ago.

The decision which was originally made concerning the appropriate level of payment was a shot in the dark, as there were no precedents. It appears to have been fairly realistic. One placement is conceived as meriting a half-time salary, two placements a full-time salary.

THE BOYS AND GIRLS IN PLACEMENT

From the start the project tried very hard to stick to the principle of a 'deep-end strategy' – to place only the 'most difficult' adolescents and to aim at a large number of placements rather than to try a few 'easy' ones first.

Lynn, a 'casualty of the system', was practically the first

referral. She was almost 16 and had been living in an assessment centre for some months. She and five of her six brothers and sisters had been in care for many years, following the break-up of their parents' marriage. They were scattered in various residential homes (even the twins were parted) and seldom saw each other. (For a full description of the family, see 'Westerland family', pp. 86–7.) Lynn had been assessed as educationally subnormal and maladjusted. She had lived in a series of foster-homes and residential centres. Her last placement had been in a boarding school for disturbed and backward girls, from which she had been expelled after attacking the staff. In the assessment centre she sat with her chin digging into her chest, her pretty face quite hidden by her hair, and refused to speak to strangers. At other times she would shout at people, The foster-parents had heard of Lynn's tragic family and were determined to get through to her. In fact, her foster-father's coaxing quite soon elicited a response. The introduction was abrupt. After several refusals, Lynn agreed to go to tea and then refused to go back to the assessment centre.

The next hurdle was school. When she was being introduced to the carefully chosen school the headmaster asked her to remove a ring. That was the end of school; she ran away and was found by her foster-parents in a telephone kiosk. Finally, individual tuition was arranged for the few remaining months of compulsory education.

Lynn changed tremendously in placement, becoming bright and sociable, but there were problems. She found it extremely difficult to start work because she was anxious and employers were put off by her rudeness and low intelligence. She finally decided that she wanted to live with her own relatives. This was a disaster. She returned to the foster-home, tried independence again and is now happily married.

The particular skill of these foster-parents was their obvious commitment to the girl. They gave her a great deal of care and attention, which she had never experienced before, coaxing her to talk and listening, remaining calm and affectionate *but not giving in* when she behaved badly.

In placing young children in 'substitute-home' foster-care, it is usually considered important that the introduction should be a slow and gradual process, so that the child is not frightened by a sudden change and the foster parents have time to learn to know him before reaching the final decision. Although these arguments are valid, the protracted process is inevitably unsettling and anxiety-provoking. For adolescents gradual introductions are not usually appropriate. To most of them their present situation is unsatisfactory, and they want an *immediate* change. If it is delayed, they may get into further trouble or run away. They always say that the introductory visits are of limited value: 'Everyone is on their best behaviour. You cannot feel what a family is like until you live there.' It is extremely counter-productive to build up anxiety by rehearsing possible difficulties, although there should be careful discussion of the rights and obligations of all concerned. The message is: 'It will be difficult, but we will help you.' As a transfer can be arranged if the match is not right, the risks are far less grave than in the case of young children in 'substitute homes'.

A foster-parent describes how one placement began:

He came to us at Easter, a 16-year-old lad with family problems and a list of offences behind him ranging from arson, burglary, robbery and theft. There was no time for the normal preliminaries. He was locked in a remand centre run by the Prison Service after absconding from a children's home and offending repeatedly whilst 'on the run'. The offences were severe, and thousands of pounds of damage and stolen goods were involved. We met him in court and persuaded the Bench to let him return to us, pending the hearing of the various offences. He had, at this time, already been in a detention centre and had, a few months previously, appeared at Crown Court with several Borstal recommendations. The judge had decided to put off sentencing him for six months to see if he had 'seen the light'. During that time he ran riot, taking us back to where we found him. It was not the happiest of Easters for any of us, least of all him, bewildered, not really understanding what was happening or where he was going. He was morose and unhappy.

He worked hard to fit, and he did, he became a part of our lives and we respected and admired him for his efforts. Eventually he found a job and worked hard at it, and was dismissed upon telling them of the three court appearances due that week and one the following week. As a family we were furious at the injustice of this – 'Judge him please as you find him, not on past history.' He took it calmly and in his stride. Rough justice was part of his life, but to us it was a vital blow, because prior to this we had to return to Crown Court, and although he had obviously broken the 'good behaviour' stipulation, the judge was induced again to postpone sentence until all the cases against him had been heard. Without the project this would not have been possible, and our first glimmer of optimism shone.

The judge obviously wanted to see what the project could do, and at last we had some time to prove that he had decided to turn over a new leaf. But now we had the disaster of no job. 'Yellow Pages' in hand, we just telephoned through alphabetically, and he went for an interview, started work immediately and has worked since. His immediate superior was aware of some of the problems, and he was allowed time off to attend the countless court sessions, and eventually the day dawned in August for the reappearance at Crown Court. We went with three new Borstal recommendations and countless other offences, and a great deal of trepidation. We spoke to the judge of the fact he had not offended at all during the time with us, that he had worked hard, that he was a pleasure to have at home. We stressed the project and the support it gave us all. After hearing all the evidence, reading countless reports, the judge went off to deliberate. His verdict was this – a bind-over for one year to be on good behaviour, and a very substantial amount of compensation to be paid. Eureka! No Borstal, and a chance for the lad to prove to the world that he really means to settle and work and love, laugh and cry like the rest of us. A big thank you to the project and the judge, a happy ending that we all hope will stretch on over the years ahead of us.

With most placements the worst time is at the beginning; with others the main storms come later, as the story of Anne (written by her foster-mother) shows. Anne was 16 years old when she was placed and almost 18 when she left. She had previously spent two years in a closed unit for girls, under considerable medication.

It is with difficulty that I try to describe what it is like to live with a very disturbed and violent adolescent.

In the beginning our foster-daughter showed little of the distress and anger which plagued her. Certainly, she lacked the polish that our six other children had learned from infancy; the unsuspecting telephone caller would have his eardrum shattered by Anne screaming for Mum to come and take a call; our friends would suffer the same treatment at the door; but she learned. She is naturally a very noisy and manic person; she craved constantly for physical demonstrations of affection, usually at the most inconvenient moments.

The other children accepted both her and her lack of basic knowledge of simple, socially acceptable behaviour and went out of their way to forgive her things that they would not have tolerated in one another.

The first signs of her violence were shown when she went to the local police station to throw stones at the windows; this heralded the end of the eight-to-ten-week 'honeymoon' period. A little later she assaulted a policeman and was taken to court. Later still she was taken to court again for abusive behaviour to the police, and at last seemed to grasp that she might be taken away from us if she continued with her 'hate the police' campaign. (I should add that at about this time Anne 'ran away' and was brought home by two handsome young policemen, who spent the car journey chatting to her, and their kindness and concern probably had a strong effect on her attitude to the police force from then on.) She resented paying the small fine imposed on her and only did so when she received a letter giving her seven days or she would be arrested.

Shortly after this she made her first attack on one of her foster-brothers, kicking him in the chest, etc. During the next six months or so she made numerous attacks on everyone in the house, with two interesting exceptions. She never attacked me and always came with tears and clinging hugs to be forgiven. I think she gave me the role of the mother she never had. I can't tell if she loves me or not. I suspect that she cannot experience love as most of us can; the damage done to her as a child seems to have arrested her emotional development. The other exception was my seven-year-old mentally handicapped daughter, to whom she was constantly kind, with rare moments of verbal teasing.

The effect of her constant physical attacks and even more constant bouts of screaming and swearing at one or another of the other children, their friends, her foster-father and most of my long-suffering friends and their children was as follows. Foster-father was the first to show stress and talk of her leaving us. This was followed by the slow death of his very real affection for her and ended with his rewarding her violence with his own. Finally he withdrew and tried to ignore her. Our 18-year-old son remained detached from her for the 16 months that she was with us. He neither liked nor disliked her. He found her intellectually boring and her behaviour incomprehensible, but accepted her as part of our family with ease. She only attacked him twice, and he found that judo was a very effective method of self-defence.

Our eldest daughter is now 16. She and Anne had a very good relationship, but Anne suffered bouts of jealousy and would hit, kick or try to strangle her foster-sister with her hair, etc. Slowly this girl's liking for, and friendship with, Anne declined. There were times when she hated Anne and said so. Today she feels sorrow for Anne and is happy for her to remain part of our family as long as she isn't living here.

Our twin sons are 14, and I think their feelings for her are fairly alike. They liked her; they were amused and interested in her highly coloured stories. They were both subjected to a lot of violence from her, some of which they deserved, being unable to keep quiet, and some of which was totally unprovoked. When we first talked of her moving on they voted that she stay. As her violence increased, we saw that one twin was beginning to emulate her behaviour in some respects, notably bad language and back-chat and resistance to any request. The other one, I suspect, became afraid of her. They have lost their warmer feelings for her but are happy for her to stay part of the family on a looser basis. You might say that their feelings became neutralized.

Our 13-year-old daughter always liked Anne. She suffered a lot of violence but consistently forgave Anne. She was relieved when Anne left but at the same time she was unhappy that she had to go. She would be happy for Anne to come back, providing the violence ceased.

Our youngest daughter is seven. She loves Anne but the outbursts of violence terrified her. She would cower in a corner, shivering, with a look of pure terror in her face, and would refuse to go near her for an hour or two afterwards.

For myself, I still love Anne and would have her back if it weren't for the others. The power of her unrecognized (by her) assaults on my emotions through the other people I love was monstrous. I found towards the end that I would tremble physically and that the loss of peace of mind left me constantly tired.

Anne was quite unable to cope with her emotions towards people whom she regarded as being peripheral to the family. Of these a young woman, a depressive who has lived with us for three years, is one. Anne felt that a 25-year-old should leave the home, and her hatred and anger towards her developed beyond reason.

As a family Anne brought us closer together. She made my children value things which most people never think about. Each small step forward for her was a step for us. She showed us the frightening, dark side of the human mind, took away our human dignity and made us afraid not so much of the actual violence but afraid in anticipation. I hope we gave her happiness and comfort. Certainly, she has left an indelible mark, to a greater or lesser degree, on each one of us and in a strange way has given our friends a greater perception of their own emotions.

I think everyone has forgiven her for her violence, but most people are wary of being put into a position where they might suffer at her hands again.

As a family we have agreed to stand by her as 'family' for as long as she likes, but not on terms which include continual violence.

Postscript During the six weeks since Anne left she has had a very short and stormy stay in a residential girls' home. Whilst there she ran home twice and kept in touch with us by telephone. She was very unhappy. As a last resort she was found a bed-sitter. Her whole attitude has changed, her telephone calls are warm and cheerful. She is coping with day-to-day problems and is coming to stay with us soon. She seems to have found her place as a nearly grown-up woman both with the family and in the world. We are again daring to believe that there is a future, that for Anne there is hope.

This is Anne's view of her experience with the family exactly as she wrote it, except that some spelling mistake: have been corrected:

I was with [the project family] for about 16 months and thanks to them all I am today living in a bed-sitter and making a life of my own. They helped me to understand some of the things that people can't or don't know how to help or understand.

They made it important that I learn love and still do. [The project family's children] all thought of me as a sister and they gave to me. I took and gave not much back to them. It was children at school that talked about things they learnt and did until I decided I had wasted [time?] at school, so I decided to go to college which I still do.

Mr — hit me when I really asked for it. He taught some respect for adults, things people didn't or don't teach me.

I think if the world had more people like [the project family] in the world the world would be a world of care and love.

I am deeply sorry about the end of living with [the project family] but I know from going to [a residential establishment]. They hid [hit?] me and some of the things I have been dish out at the [?] should not go on, from now on I will never hit with fists or bottle etc., from now on until I die, I swear.

Anne continued her successful, independent life. She remains in close contact with her foster-family and married from their house. The secret of the success of this placement was the foster-mother's loving acceptance of Anne and the normal, loving family life with which she was surrounded. Anne had been rejected by her own family, and such persistent affection, even after quarrels, was a new experience for her.

Boys as well as girls can be violent; but where boys are concerned violence is generally mixed with delinquent behaviour, which brings them into contact with the police. Jim was placed when he was almost 16. He had been made the subject of a care order two years before after three convictions for 'highway robbery' offences. (He still maintains that he was innocent of one of them.)

Both Jim's parents have worked very hard to reach their present fairly affluent position, and there is no other delinquency in the family. Jim's troubles began after his father returned from the army. He began to truant from school and to choose delinquent companions. After the care order he was admitted to a community home for boys and attended the local secondary school. He did not go to school regularly and disliked the home, in particular the superintendent, with whom he was in constant conflict. He embarked on large-scale fraud and theft as an act of defiance. He said he was going to show 'them' that he could 'beat the system'. When his crimes were discovered he was remanded in custody until his case could be heard by the Crown Court, with a recommendation for Borstal. At that point he was referred to the project and offered the choice of foster-care with an unknown family or Borstal, subject to the Court's agreement. He chose fostering, and the family also agreed to take an unknown boy. The judge deferred sentence for five months.

Jim settled down at once with the family, which had a small farm. For the eight weeks until he was old enough to enter employment he worked on the farm without payment and then found himself a job. He did not offend again, and after about 12 months in placement (a period agreed between Jim, his parents and his foster-parents) will return to live with his own parents.

The foster-family were successful with Jim, but they worked for it. He was almost unbelievably unrealistic; he lived in a world of dramatic fantasies and had constantly to be 'talked down' into reality. On the other hand, he was a kind and friendly boy, willing to work hard and even at jobs he did not like. The foster-family and his own family had a generally friendly relationship, although the foster-family exerted quite strong pressure on the parents to insist on Jim's becoming more reliable.

Jim did not want to 'beat the system' in foster-care, and he genuinely tried to improve. The skill of the foster-parents lay in their endless 'talking down', in their provision of appropriate occupation (Jim loved animals) and their close work with the parents.

Finally, sexual problems are certainly easier to deal with in foster-care than in a residential unit. Foster-mothers, who themselves probably attend the Family Planning Clinic, can help girls to work out what kind of sexual person they want to be and to control their fertility efficiently. This is essentially a one-person job, part of a close and trusting relationship. The contraceptive pill is tremendously helpful in 'buying time' for promiscuous young girls, who tend to settle down after a while and cease to need contraceptives until they begin to develop more mature sexual relationships.

Boys also have sexual problems; again, these are certainly

easier to deal with in a foster-family. In the intimate environment of a family, sexual problems tend to come to the surface more quickly than in a group situation.

One boy was placed after three years in a residential home for boys, where he had been labelled as a homosexual. He had stolen quite a lot of female underwear, but nobody had spoken to him of this. The underwear had simply been removed from his suitcase without a word, so he had spent a lot of time wondering who knew and what was going to happen now that he had been found out. It is interesting that this topic cropped up almost as soon as he was introduced to a family, and he seemed to experience tremendous relief in being able to discuss sexual matters after the silence of the residential home. Although he still has problems with sexual identity, he is with a family which answers his questions, dispelling the fears and fantasies he had before. He feels he is able to ask questions without being afraid of being considered stupid or wondering what others might think.

Iris Murdoch, in describing how she writes, spoke of 'tearing away the veil of fantasy, in order to be able to see reality'.[3] This would be a good description of an important part of the adolescent's work during a placement. George Lyward used to talk about 'stern love' – love which is totally honest but never rejects, is compassionate but never dodges the harsh and inconsistent demands of reality. This stands in contrast to the attitudes of some social workers, who may try to establish or maintain relationships by buying adolescents alcohol or cigarettes, by condoning activites which are against the law and by dodging the pain of reality. Anne-Lise Kålvesten describes the fostering method for disturbed younger children as

> regulated regression therapy plus ego-oriented demands. In the evening the little rogue can be a baby, show that he is frightened and nestle close. The foster-mother will sit beside his bed until he is asleep, or hold him on her lap until he drops off to sleep in her arms. But next morning the demands of reality are there again; the boy must get up and get dressed in order to catch the school bus, even if he has to be carried out.[4]

Add to this the skill of talking everything out as openly and frankly as possible and the foster-parents' methods are more or less described. However, in the last analysis the one thing which matters most of all with adolescents is not to give up. Nearly all of them will come through their difficulties in the end if we can only hang on long enough, without resorting to 'remedies' which make them worse.

THE FOSTER-PARENTS

There is no data at all in English on the kind of families likely to be successful in the foster-care of adolescents, except for Kålvesten's study of 40 Swedish foster-families caring for difficult adolescents, in which she describes the typical foster-family and sets her findings against the background of a much wider study of Swedish families.[5]

> Compared with the whole Swedish population, the foster-family was of a clearly distinguishable sociological type: living in the country or in small places. Self-employed people with wives working at home, orderly economy but seldom any real wealth. Age-wise spread over a broad scale with the majority having their own children who were now grown up or teenagers.
>
> However, the group also comprised other types, where the husband and sometimes also the wife were employed in various occupations, where the parents were quite young and where the natural children were small . . . one man and one woman were single foster-parents. Nothing indicated that these more varied types of families were less equipped to handle the children they had been allotted. And that is an encouraging thought with regard to the future.
>
> When we look at the internal family situation, the foster-family was compared with a group of randomly selected Stockholm families. The most significant difference was that all married men and women in the foster-home group considered that they had a good marriage. The majority also had a more positive attitude towards their childhood homes and towards the upbringing they had received than was the case with the control group. On this point there were however also exceptions and we called them miracles, as these people had done something good with their lives despite a miserable start.

If our finds are pointing in the right direction, it would then be right to look for foster-parents for difficult children among people whom we have generally seen to be satisfied with themselves and their conditions and at the same time are armed with some type of surplus – of human interest, energy, mental capacity, intelligence and, last but not least, time. All these being resources of which they do not make full use until they get a difficult foster-child. Such a surplus can most often be found with people who think that they have succeeded well with bringing up their own children. It is, however, important to state that the same surplus sometimes is available in families with small children and with people without children.

These Swedish families were confident in their own abilities and able, for that reason, to help their foster-children. It is also interesting to note that, by comparison with other families, a high proportion of these foster-families' own parents had been active in their community or church. There was a tradition of public service. Many of Kålvesten's observations were also true of the project's foster-parents, and the points she makes about positive attitudes towards their own lives and the concept of a 'surplus' are particularly important.

Foster-parents in the project ranged in age from their mid-twenties to their early sixties, with young or grown-up children or no children. They were married or divorced. Two divorced women and one widow acted as single parents, but no single women or single or divorced men applied.

No foster-parents were very rich and none were very poor. None of the husbands were unskilled and most held professional posts of various kinds. Not all wives had had particularly skilled or responsible jobs, but all of them had worked and had enjoyed the experience. As with the husbands there was a wide and interesting range of careers. Only 26 per cent of the families were members of any religious denomination. Perhaps the most striking point is that the vast majority of families were buying their own home and for this reason a second income was very important.

Project foster-parents tended to be energetic, outgoing people, good verbalizers who could discuss difficult matters openly with adolescents. They were generally practical and capable. They regarded themselves as the adolescent's champions and would take endless trouble to pursue what they considered to be the children's rights or best interests.

The other side of this coin was that they were often sharply critical of what they viewed as unreasonable bureaucratic delays or obstacles. They expected efficient administrative

Table 3.2
Foster-families with at least one project placement

	No. of families (total 74)
Age (total divided by 2)	
21–30 years	7
31–40 years	35
41–50 years	25
51–60 years	7
No. of children	
0	5
1	9
2	28
3	15
4	15
4+	2
Experience of fostering	
Families with previous experience of fostering	13
Families caring for a non-project foster child	4
Housing	
Own house	65
Council house	4
Rented accommodation	2
Vicarage	3
Location	
Country	32
Suburb	12
Town	30
Religion	
Active	19
Non-active	55

Table 3.3
(a) *Occupations of project foster-fathers**

Professional and executive	22	Workshop supervisor	1
		Farmer	1
Engineer	8	Pilot	1
Social worker	6	Hairdresser	1
Teacher	5	Butcher	1
Own business	4	Builder	1
Retired	3	Miner	1
Salesman	2	Compositor	1
Carpenter	2	Seaman	1
Driver	2	Other skilled trades	7
Site foreman	1		

*Total 71, as three families had no foster-father.

(b) *Occupations of project foster-mothers*

It was not easy to compile data on the wives' careers, as some of them had been housewives for a number of years. However, it was quite clear that as a group they had been employed in a wide range of occupations and had enjoyed working. The largest group had been secretaries (12) and nurses (11). The next two largest groups were teachers (6) and residential social workers (6), followed by field social workers (3) and youth workers (3). Among the others there were a psychologist, an actress, a builder, a librarian, an hotelier, an upholsterer, an accountant and one woman who ran her own business, and a number of wives had worked, regularly or intermittently, in factories and domestic employment of various kinds.

practices and were quick to criticize social work which did not appear to produce results. There was a tendency for these criticisms to become reinforced during group discussions if several families had had unsatisfactory experiences.

Among the people who applied for this work with adolescents there were very few traditional foster-parents; of those who did apply several were dissatisfied with the traditional fostering role, feeling that too little was expected of them by the social workers.

Social workers sometimes questioned the suitability of project families who had no 'experience' or 'qualifications'. Hessen's experience (and our own) suggests that people who do not hold any relevant qualifications are just as successful as 'qualified' people.[6] The evaluation of the Hessen project also showed that people with a 'socio-political' motivation were less likely to be successful than those who simply liked children and adolescents. Some German practitioners suggest that highly qualified families may on occasions be unsuccessful 'because they will not leave the children alone'. In the project previous experience of fostering or of working with adolescents was certainly useful but did not appear to be a prerequisite for success. Experience of traditional fostering had little relevance to adolescent placements, as the placement of younger children rests on the view that adults must know what is best for the child, who is too young to judge for himself. The treatment placement of adolescents is based on the assumption that the adolescent is old enough to think for himself and to agree to a plan of working designed to resolve the problems which he can acknowledge.

Both husbands and wives played an important part in the placement, but whereas the wives were always 'front-line workers' *vis à vis* the adolescent, there appeared to be three roles for the foster-father. In some families the husband worked very long hours, sometimes commuting to London. His role was crucial in supporting his wife rather than in offering much direct help to the adolescent. Other husbands worked away from home but were very much involved in the placement when they were there. Finally, some husbands worked from their own home, running a farm or a business, and gave as much direct help to the adolescent as did their wives (in some instances even more).

Although the foster-parents' marriages were almost invariably secure and well-established, this did not mean that the husband and wife always agreed. In some cases, where two strong and extremely different people were married to each other, the resulting dissonance, far from upsetting the adolescent, seemed to help by producing a measure of tension, which promoted different viewpoints but was not overwhelming. For example, in one family the wife's gentle, loving idealism was counterbalanced by her husband's responses, which were considerably less tolerant and much fiercer but realistic and not rejecting.

Two marriages broke down while the family had a project placement, and a divorce followed. In one case the placement was made in the knowledge that the marriage was at risk because the family could help the adolescent enter a specific career. In the second instance the divorce followed 22 years of marriage and was caused by the husband's transfer to a new job in another country. Both the project placements and the adolescent children of the family were upset, but it is difficult to see how an event of this kind could possibly have been predicted.

In general, the health of the foster-families was good. One father did not work because of a permanent disability. Several people had operations of various kinds (one was very unsuccessful). One foster-mother was admitted to a psychiatric hospital for a brief period.

With such a wide range of foster parents it is difficult to put flesh on the bare statistical bones by means of a pen picture. However, here are two examples of experienced families who worked with the project from the time it started and took a series of placements.

Mr and Mrs White own their own house in a seaside town. Mr White runs his own business from home; Mrs White used to work in an office. They have a married daughter, who often visits them, and a son, aged 19, who is on the brink of leaving home. They have always been active members of the local community, with a special interest in youth and handicapped people. Taking adolescent placements has provided them with a career in their own home, which they can share and which carries status and a reasonable financial reward. They enjoy the work, which has broadened their role in the community and has given them the satisfaction of considerable success.

Their semi-detached house is beautifully furnished and equipped, extremely neat and spotlessly clean. The house is full of jokes and laughter, and everyone leads a very full social life. However, quite formal family discussions are held about all important matters, and when rules have been agreed, they are very strictly enforced. The natural parents of adolescents placed with Mr and Mrs White can readily understand and co-operate with this kind of 'treatment'.

Mr and Mrs Brown are buying a large house in the country. They have five children of their own and a boy and girl from the project. In addition, there are always other people staying in the house and a wide range of animals wandering about. The house is always untidy and mealtimes are erratic. Mr Brown works long hours commuting to London and can be roused to anger by adolescent bad behaviour. His wife is more patient and persistent in talking out problems. The whole family is a truly caring community, where no one is rejected or ignored, however awful his behaviour may be.

In the four and a half years under review 26 families took a placement and subsequently dropped out. Two of these families dropped out within a few weeks, shortly after the start of the project, and can be excluded on the grounds that they did not fully understand what they were undertaking. Another family withdrew but may continue in the future. The reasons for the other 23 dropouts are shown in table 3.4.

Of the seven families who did not request another placement, one had problems at home and one wife was in full-time employment. Two of the others continued to

Table 3.4
Withdrawals from the project

Cause	No. of families
Moved to another area	4
Death or illness	2
Change in family circumstances: new baby, arrival of grandparent, divorce (2)	4
Changed to fostering handicapped children	1
Planned to start group home	1
Returned to residential child care	1
Did not request a further placement (i.e. not motivated to continue)	7
Project not prepared to offer another placement, for specific reasons	2
Children of family objected	1

provide an active after-care service for their ex-placement, and two families had worked hard for the project for almost five years and felt that they needed a rest. They continued to attend the group and to help in various ways. Thus even the families who gave up working for the project were in most instances not dissatisfied with the work *per se*.

Once families had joined a group, very few dropped out either before or after a placement had been made, except when changes in their circumstances forced them to withdraw. On a few occasions a family visited a group once or twice and then withdrew. (These included a couple of divisional foster-parents who decided against transferring to the project.) One of the crucial factors in the success of the project was the high morale of the families and the stability of the groups. There was a tremendous commitment to what was perceived as a very important and challenging task, which went far beyond the immediate work of caring for an individual adolescent and created the feeling that all the foster-families were taking part in a campaign or crusade on behalf of mistreated young people.

Although very few families dropped out and the loyalty to, and enthusiasm for, the project was striking, one considerable worry remained and even increases from year to year. After four years a foster-family might have completed as many as four placements. In many instances, the adolescent has remained permanently attached to the family, like a young adult son or daughter who is warmly welcomed at weekends and at Christmas. In addition, the family has provided a good deal of advice and practical help. All this has been undertaken willingly and, at the time of writing, generally without any remuneration. But apart from the pressures on space, an after-care service of this kind inevitably involves the family in expense – sometimes quite heavy in the case of weddings and other celebrations. With a family's own children there is a natural limit, but with foster-children the effect snowballs. Of course, the boys and girls generally make a contribution themselves, but this does not meet the expense fully. As this voluntary after-care service is often crucial to the long-term success or failure of the adolescent, some way needs to be found of ensuring that foster-families do not suffer financially, although this would not solve the problems of space and possible emotional over-burdening.

Conclusion

There did not seem to be a 'standard' pattern of foster-care. Adolescents who had suffered from lack of control in their own homes sometimes appeared to welcome an extremely controlling relationship with their foster-parents, provided that this was combined with a rich and enjoyable shared social life. Several of the project families operated in this way, but the foster-parents were not 'authoritarian' figures because the 'treatment pattern' was shared and agreed with the adolescent. (The Hessen evaluation showed that authoritarian foster-parents tended to fail; see p. 148.) Other families were extremely loving and permissive and equally successful. The crucial point was a successful match between adolescent and family.

For some divisional social workers a difficulty appeared to be that social-work training had developed an inner model of what foster-parents ought to be like, based on experience of the placement of younger children, and the project families were judged by these criteria. The project believed that the only criteria by which they should be judged was whether or not they could contribute to solving the adolescents' problems. Whether the project workers or the divisional social workers *liked* these families was immaterial as long as the adolescents in their homes liked them and made good progress.

The project workers were asked what they looked for when they recruited families. They could not give a satisfactory answer, as there was no reliable body of knowledge to tell us what to look for or how to recognize it when we saw it. No applicants were rejected, except those who were ruled out for quite specific reasons, such as health or criminal convictions. The families then had to survive the group process and some spent months (even a year) in the group before an appropriate match was agreed.

In retrospect, however, it seems that certain qualities were essential. Families had to be able to communicate openly and honestly; they had to be able to learn; and they needed considerable emotional resilience.

THE FAMILIES OF ORIGIN

During the course of the project 144 families were studied (in a number of cases several children from the same family had been placed). In two instances absolutely nothing was known about the family of origin. Information about the parents' marital status was fairly complete, as it affected the legal status of their children, and information about the ages of most of them was available. But information about housing and occupation was very incomplete. It was difficult to tell whether families lived in council houses or rented accommodation – and, of course, they often moved. Similarly, information about occupation was scanty and inaccurate because parents were often unemployed or changed jobs. Sometimes data on 'fathers' related to stepfathers, sometimes to natural fathers. However, if the information is considered as a whole, a picture of the families' way of life does emerge (see table 3.5). It is quite obvious that these figures for the marital status of the parents of origin are not representative of the population as a whole, and they are in stark contrast to the stability of the foster-parents' marriages. It is equally obvious that the adolescents had had very difficult situations to cope with in their own families.

Table 3.5
Structure of project families of origin

	No. of families
Mother dead	3
Father dead	7
Both parents dead	6
Single unmarried mother	14
Parents divorced or separated	69
Parents married and living together	43

The age scatter of the parents of origin presents a very clear picture, even though the information is incomplete in some cases. If the ages of both parents at placement are added (where possible) and divided by two, it is quite clear that most were within the range between the late thirties and the late forties (see table 3.6). No parent was under 30, and only a minority were over 50. The ages of deceased parents have not been included.

Table 3.6
Ages of parents of origin

Age range (total divided by 2)	No. of families
31–40 years	59
41–50 years	62
51–60 years	12

Figure 3.1 (a) shows the pattern of family size, which includes a disproportionate number of large families and represents a considerable contrast to figure 3.1 (b), for foster families. Six of the eight children who had no siblings were the illegitimate offspring of unmarried women. Some of the families were very large indeed, including one family with 13 children and another with ten.

It is difficult to make an accurate statement about housing as the files do not always indicate the type of housing and also because some of the families are very mobile. However, it is clear that families of origin occupy council houses much more often than the foster-families and are rather more likely to live in towns.

The 'father's occupation' was derived from the information given about the 'family home' (the house in which the father or stepfather was living with the mother). No attempt was made to include the occupation of separated or divorced fathers. The occupations covered a wide range, from a well-to-do company director to unskilled labourers in intermittent employment (see table 3.7).

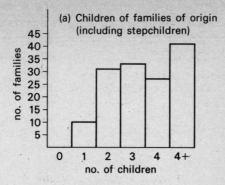

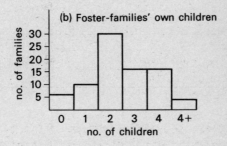

Figure 3.1
Natural and foster-families: comparison of size

There were thus 27 unskilled men among the families of origin and none among the foster-families. It is also interesting to note that members of the forces were represented in this group but not among the foster-parents. (The number of fathers in the services is rather under-represented in this list as several more had only recently left the forces. If this group is added to the drivers, there is quite a large number of fathers who tended to be away from home.) Sentences of imprisonment could not be accurately counted, but a substantial number of fathers had been in prison. Some fathers had also been admitted to psychiatric hospitals, so that the chances of the father's absence from home were higher than average.

Table 3.7
Occupations of fathers of origin

Professional and executive	6
Own business	4
Skilled trades	32
Armed forces or merchant marine	6
Drivers	7
Unskilled	27

A large proportion of mothers did not go out to work or worked intermittently, but in many cases both parents were working, and sometimes adolescent children were also in employment. The mothers' employment also covered a wide range. For example, there were in full-time employment two teachers, a secretary, a bookshop owner, a receptionist and a laboratory technician, but there were also unskilled factory workers and cleaners, often working part-time. Four mothers were long-term psychiatric in-patients.

From the information available on the files it is not possible to make an accurate statement about the health of the families of origin, but there are repeated references to admissions to general or psychiatric hospitals or to chronic states of ill-health, such as arthritis, depression, alcoholism and so on.

As with the foster-families, it is difficult to give a representative picture of the families of origin, but two examples illustrate how different they could be.

Mr and Mrs Westerland were both children of large, working-class families. They married young, and seven children were born of the marriage. They were very poor and lived in overcrowded, rented accommodation. The marriage was not a happy one and was characterized by a great deal of physical violence. Finally, the parents separated, and all the children except the youngest one came into care. The three boys were placed together in a children's home a considerable distance away from their parents and remained there for many years. The three girls did not remain together. They were fostered several times, but on each occasion the arrangement quickly broke down because of their difficult

behaviour, so that they were transferred to various institutions for disturbed or maladjusted children. Both parents
lived rather unsettled lives with a series of partners, but the
father was in regular employment and kept in touch with the
children.

At the age of 15 Lynn Westerland was expelled from a
residential school for maladjusted girls following uncontroll-
able behaviour culminating in an attack on the staff. She was
educationally backward and very surly (see page 65). She
was placed in a foster-home within easy reach of both parents
and maintained an affectionate relationship with her father.
The re-introduction to her mother was less successful and
ended in a fist fight in the street. The sisters in this family were
very attached to one another and kept in touch without
prompting, but the brothers had drifted away, only retaining
contact with the father.

Mr and Mrs Leroy lived in a charming old house in a
pleasant village. Mr Leroy held a well-paid executive
position, and they were buying their own home. They had two
adopted children, James and Bettina. Bettina was a pretty,
fair-haired girl, and by the age of 12 had become the family
favourite. She was obedient, affectionate and generally
popular.

By the age of 15 James's situation was very bad. His own
parents were not English, and by adolescence his appearance
had become clearly foreign and unlike that of his parents and
sister. He began to carry out various break-ins and burglaries,
and relationships at home were tense. On one occasion he hit
his mother. Neither parent was able to come close to James or
to understand his point of view, and a referral to the Child
Guidance Clinic achieved nothing. The family was very
ashamed of James's delinquency and rebuffed friendly offers
of help. A supervision order made by the juvenile court did
not appear to affect the situation at all.

Finally, a care order was made, and James was sent to the
closed section of a community home with education (he was
supposed to be violent). He spent a year there. When the
community home wanted him to leave, he was referred to the
project. His assessment form mentioned psychopathic tend-
encies. He was placed after a very brief introduction and is a

gentle and loving boy.

Meanwhile, his parents had moved to another area. They had had little contact with him during his stay in the closed unit and, once away from the area, contact diminished to occasional letters.

Conclusion

There is no escaping the conclusion that the family circumstances of the adolescents were unfavourable. They were likely to have come to the project from broken or extremely large families, or their fathers may have been away from home. There was a fairly high incidence of psychiatric and physical illness in their families.

For this group housing conditions and poverty were rather less of a problem than for the families of younger children in care. Although some families were very poor, they often had two adult earners and sometimes one or two adolescents also in employment. A substantial number of families had a high standard of living.

The difficulties which the adolescents encountered in their own families were therefore on the whole due less to socio-economic factors than to interpersonal stress or lack of parental interest. In most cases it was unlikely that this situation could have been substantially improved by increasing the parental income.

4 The Project in Action: Outside the Families

PUBLIC RELATIONS

Our knowledge of the way in which both workers and youths in Massachusetts had collaborated with the media in their campaign to close the training schools for young delinquents encouraged us to seek the co-operation of the media from the very start.[1]

When the project was set up the general climate of opinion among social workers was that no families would be willing to take into their homes disturbed or delinquent adolescents. The general public appeared to accept institutional care as the obvious response to adolescent problems – not surprisingly, in view of England's long tradition of boarding schools for the children of the rich. It was therefore clear that there was a double-sided problem: to educate the public and to recruit foster-families. The project strategy was to recruit families by explaining to the public, as loudly as possible, the nature of the problem and what the project wanted to offer as a solution.

When work started in January 1975 the first tasks were to obtain an office, a secretary and the necessary equipment. This took a considerable time. This period was also used to make contact with the divisions and residential establishments. As soon as these preliminaries were more or less complete, a press conference was held, in April 1975, to launch the scheme.

The county public relations officer invited the national and local press and national and local television and radio. The chairman of Kent County Council Social Services Committee, Mrs Dorothy Elvy, the Director of Social

Services, Nicolas Stacey, and the project organizer all spoke briefly and responded to questions. Emphasis was placed on the importance of a new approach to teenage problems. The meeting was very well attended and was followed by coverage at national and local level in the press and on radio and television. As a result of this meeting, 60 families wrote to inquire about the project.

A year later a second press conference was held, at which the chairman, the director, the project organizer and a foster-father spoke briefly, and other families were present to talk with the reporters. Again, we were fortunate in our coverage in the media. This time some of the adolescents spoke to reporters and appeared on television.

A third press conference was held in 1977, but considerably fewer reporters attended, although some contacted the project organizer and reports did appear in the media. It was felt that the project was now too well-established for further press conferences to be useful.

Apart from the reporting which followed the press conferences, the project always welcomed reporters, and the families and adolescents were pleased to talk to them. As a result, a steady stream of articles and features appeared in the national and local press, in women's magazines and in social-work periodicals, and in 1977 an independent television company made an hour-long film of three placements, entitled *Peter, Tina and Steve*. It was directed by Lord Snowdon and is a beautiful and accurate film. Social workers, adolescents, foster-families and the parents of origin all participated willingly.

This exercise in public relations had two important results. First, the project had no difficulties in recruiting families. No advertisement ever appeared and no recruitment campaigns were undertaken. However, as the size of the project increased, recruitment took place more and more through the recommendations of existing families. Second, we were obliged to reconsider traditional ideas on confidentiality. Too much emphasis appears to have been placed by social workers on the concept of confidentiality. People seem to welcome the opportunity to tell interested strangers about their problems. Of course, there are perils, and it is possible that the excitement of the film had a rather unbalancing effect on one of the boys who appeared in it, but no other adverse effects were visible. Reporters always treated the project seriously and fairly.

Another aspect of the public relations exercise was the project's effort to publish as much descriptive material as possible. The team produced four progress reports, in 1976, 1977, 1978 and 1980, which gave a fairly detailed account of the work. I wrote a substantial number of articles and contributions to books describing the work of the project, and Rosemary Tozer also contributed a chapter and several articles, with particular reference to similar work in the United States. The members of the project team and both foster-parents and adolescents spoke at conferences and seminars and to groups of foster-parents and social workers in the United Kingdom and Eire, and I gave three lectures in German at Frankfurt, Tübingen and Berlin in 1979. This text was subsequently published.[2]

In conclusion, the project deliberately set out to become as public as possible in order to recruit families and to educate the public. This part of the work was extremely successful. As a result many local authorities and voluntary organizations in the United Kingdom and other countries have now set up schemes based on the Kent principles and methods.

THE SOCIAL-WORK INPUT

Any service for placing children in the community requires a substantial input of social-work time. Even if this is calculated according to the minimum requirements of the boarding-out rules, the time needed for assessing foster-homes, placing adolescents and supervising and reviewing placements is substantial.

It is difficult to make an accurate statement about the amount of social work that was required for the project placements. Theoretically, as much as possible of the work should be done by the foster-parents, and the social workers should not detract from their responsibilities as 'focal therapists'. The foster-parents consulted in times of difficulty but were expected to act and to decide for themselves. The project workers spent the equivalent of one evening per week with foster-parents in groups. The amount of time they spent with these families in their homes was influenced by the way in which responsibility was shared with the divisional social worker. Some divisional social workers used the project workers as their agents in relation to the adolescent; some did the work themselves. With adolescents and project families much of the work could be done by telephone, which saved a great deal of time and travel. (Experience has shown that in a large county a project worker can build up to a maximum caseload of 15 to 18 current cases and two groups.)

Transfer of assumptions
There were some difficulties in breaking with traditional fostering practices, which were inappropriate. One problem was that families who had previously operated as traditional foster-parents sometimes expected social workers to make arrangements on their behalf or over-consulted; social workers might act as go-betweens between the project family and the family of origin or might compete with the foster-parents for the role of 'focal therapist' in respect of the adolescent.

A second problem was related to the issue of introductions. Reference has already been made to the fact that long introductions may be inappropriate for adolescents (see p. 66), and many of the successful Swedish placements of disturbed older children were made very fast.[3] Divisional social workers were, however, sometimes unwilling to deviate from the 'received wisdom', which recommends a gradual process of introduction.

The placement of adolescents is inevitably different from boarding-out younger children. With a younger child any mistake in placing is likely to have irrevocable consequences. With an adolescent it is possible to negotiate a re-placement and to turn this experience into a specific piece of social education.

There is some knowledge based on research and some rather ill-defined assumptions based on practice which seem to constitute a sort of rule book on fostering. Almost all this 'knowledge' is based on the experience of providing 'substitute homes' for younger children. The number of adolescents placed after their fourteenth birthday has always been small and very little has been written about these placements, but it is clear that 'treatment' homes for adolescents seem to require different qualities in foster-parents from those sought in 'substitute homes' for younger children.

Interpretation of data
The second area where differences between the project's approach and traditional attitudes were evident was the interpretation of data. The project believed that the adolescents and families generally said what they meant and that it was important to develop open and frank communication. The project workers did not believe that they possessed the key to hidden or unconscious meanings, although those could well have existed. The point is important, as it follows that one cannot determine what course of action is best except from what the adolescents and families say (or from 'hard' data, such as illness or convictions). Any power to predict future developments is particularly limited in view of the changeable nature of adolescence.

Counselling
In traditional fostering the social worker acts as counsellor to the foster-parents and may legitimately assume the role of 'knowledgeable expert'. As there is virtually no data about 'treatment homes' for adolescents, project workers and families chose to learn together, and the groups constituted the workshops where problems and developments were discussed and where an attempt was made to evaluate progress. It is interesting that the Hessen project started by providing foster-families with fortnightly individual counselling sessions with 'experts' (psychologists and others).[4] Under pressure from the families, they moved towards a pattern of group meetings.

Accountability
The divisional social worker was legally responsible for the

welfare of the adolescent. He chose a placement through the project just as he would have chosen a residential place. He was bound to maintain a relationship of trust and friendship with the boy or girl in order that the adolescent should have an outsider in whom he or she could confide (and complain, if necessary) and so that he might assure himself that the placement had positive value for the adolescent. The divisional social worker's jurisdiction over placement in a 'treatment home' was similar to that over placement in a residential centre.

The project parents or the residential social workers are the key people *vis-à-vis* the adolescents and equal partners in the professional team offering planned care to the adolescent and his family. Each residential centre and each project family inevitably develop their own style of work.

Some of the tensions which arose in the project were similar to the misunderstandings which grow up between field and residential social workers. The following quotation from a study of residential care made by the National Children's Bureau might have been written about the project:[5]

> Staff feel that their authority in respect of the child for whom they care, which they anticipated would be substantial, suffers public reduction by the fact that their employer recognizes the field social worker and not themselves as the link between the youngster, his parents and the outside world. If the child wants to spend a night away with friends, if the child requires extra clothing, if the child wants to visit his parents, then it is the field social worker who must be consulted and whose approval must be obtained.
>
> What happens is this: you get invited to stay overnight with a friend. The staff know them and think it's all right, but they say, 'I'll have to get your social worker's permission.' Then you wait for three weeks and may be the social worker visits your friend's family to check everything's okay, may be he doesn't. Anyway after three weeks it's too late. Kids in care lose lots of friends that way. It's very hard to explain to people.

Both project families and divisional social workers were occasionally possessive about 'their' child, social workers sometimes feeling that families of origin might find it hard to communicate with project families and might therefore need an intermediary. With a few exceptions, however, the project families and families of origin found a meeting-point in shared experiences and developed quite a good working relationship in direct contact with each other. Working with the parents of adolescents was, in many ways, different from working with the ambivalent and guilt-ridden attitudes of the natural parents of younger children. However, although it was obviously easier to accept help with an adolescent whose behaviour in his own home had become impossible, the divisional social worker still had an important part to play in helping the parents of origin to overcome their feelings of guilt and shame at 'putting away' their child.

The project worker had three roles: those of recruiter, matchmaker and troubleshooter.

As recruiter, he had to find the families who would participate; ensure that the formal inquiries were completed; and ascertain that the families were enabled to discover for themselves if they wished to undertake the work and were provided with the kind of training they needed to equip themselves for the tasks ahead. The project worker ran the groups which provided training and support.

As matchmaker, the project worker studied the referrals which were made and suggested to the applicants which adolescents might best fit into their families. He was responsible for enabling introductions to take place, for working out a treatment plan, for obtaining the agreement of all parties and for writing the contracts. He was also responsible for seeing that the placement got off to a good start and was then expected to reduce his level of involvement. He arranged for the payment of the professional fee.

As troubleshooter, the project worker intervened at any point during the placement to try to resolve difficulties or deal with complaints. For out-of-hours emergencies each foster-family had their project worker's home telephone number for consultation and access to the county's 24-hour emergency service if further help was needed (until this service was suspended on 30 November 1979).

Although the role of the divisional social worker was not to provide direct treatment himself, he was responsible for submitting reliable information at the point of referral. He also retained accountability for the welfare of the adolescent, had to satisfy himself that the match was appropriate and to participate in establishing the treatment plan and in drawing up the contracts. He had to ensure that the appropriate financial and material support was available. He was expected to maintain a relationship of trust and friendship with the adolescent throughout the placement in order to make sure that a satisfactory service was provided (although it was the responsibility of the project family to carry out the treatment plan and to work with the adolescent, outside agencies, such as schools, clinics and employers, and the family of origin). Unless otherwise agreed, the divisional social worker was responsible for making the statutory visits required by the boarding-out regulations. This was an area in which it was particularly important for roles to be carefully defined, as the divisional social worker may also have been concerned with problems in the family of origin which were not directly related to the welfare of the adolescent.

The presence of two social workers had a number of advantages. In particular, it diminished the power of any one individual by ensuring that decisions were shared. It gave the adolescent a choice of outside confidant, and it enabled the social workers to help each other by standing in during holidays or absences.

Sharing care was difficult for all concerned but inevitable. In the long run, for the adolescent and his family the placement may have been only an interlude in a long history of involvement with the Social Services Department, most of which had nothing to do with the project. Conversely, for the project family a placement was perhaps one of a series, and each adolescent may have had a different social worker. One of the most difficult aspects of the work for families who entered the project was to learn to collaborate with social workers within a large bureaucracy.

Changes of social worker
One of the worst features of local authority social work is the lack of continuity caused by high staff turnover and frequent

reorganization within the social-work teams. An analysis of the first 25 project placements was made which showed that on average the adolescents had roughly one change of divisional social worker per annum. The continuity of project social workers was good for some adolescents but not for others, as each time a new project worker was appointed changes in existing caseloads were made. Some families and adolescents came off very badly, with changes of both project and divisional social worker.

Where the change of social worker was carefully planned, the effects could be minimized. Sometimes there was a long gap before the new divisional social worker was allocated. On one or two occasions he or she was unwilling to accept the current plan, which obviously caused difficulties. On other occasions a change of social worker, divisional or project, was agreed because of acute personal incompatibility between the people concerned. Changes of social worker are almost always detrimental, but the present instability reinforces the argument in favour of giving as much responsibility as possible to foster-parents. They do not usually change.

Relationships with residential establishments

During the life of the project it was not the practice for residential staff to follow their charges out into the community, this role being reserved for the field social worker.

Project workers and residential staff generally collaborated without difficulty in arranging placements – the residential staff were generally only too well aware of the limitations of institutional care and glad of the opportunity to launch the adolescent into a family. In one respect they shared a problem with the divisional social worker: both had to trust the project's assessment of a family as a suitable match. Residential and divisional social workers knew the adolescents better than the project workers, but they could not get to know the families. This was a difficult decision to share, but the fact of sharing was a safeguard for the child.

Project workers have often been asked how adolescents in residential care were prepared for placement, and the question is not easy to answer. Adolescents were asked if they would like to be fostered, and subsequent discussion included an explanation of the aims and methods of 'project fostering'. It was considered pointless to raise the level of anxiety by rehearsing all the things that could go wrong; the important point was a guarantee of help and support. (In any case, there does not seem to be any way of learning how to live in a family while living in residential care.)

Shared decision-making

The word 'share' has been used over and over again; it was fundamental to the project's mode of working.

A foster-parent could not decide unilaterally to evict a child. He had to give four weeks' notice, call a meeting of all concerned and share his ideas about the next step forward. The adolescent or the social worker had to do the same. Similarly, within the project team there was no formal individual supervision. Each member was responsible for his own work, but each decision had to be shared. (With four members the team was small enough for group supervision and decision-making.) Work with the placements was shared between the divisional social worker and the project worker.

This practice ran counter to much traditional 'case-based' social-work practice, in which the social worker who is legally accountable is considered to be in sole charge of the case, under the supervision of a superior in the hierarchy. This practice rests on the one-to-one assumptions of individual casework and supervision.

Furthermore, project practice differed sharply from traditional social work in rejecting 'expert dominance'. The project did not accept that the views of a social worker – qualified or not, whether from the project or the divisions – should constitute the last word. (Legally, however, the last word does rest with the divisional social worker, who is empowered to remove the young person at any time.) Social workers do not necessarily know best. Thus applicants had to discover for themselves whether they were suited to the work, rather than being assessed by experts, and an agreed plan had to stand unless all participants consented to changes.

The equalitarian ethos, the rejection of expert dominance and the shared decision-making of the project will make the future task of integration into the Social Services Department far from easy.

EXTERNAL RELATIONSHIPS OF THE ADOLESCENT AND PROJECT FAMILY

The adolescent in placement was the centre of a much more complex social system than the boy or girl in his own home. In figures 4.1 and 4.2 the systems are set out like the spokes of a wheel. A 'normal', non-delinquent adolescent's wheel has seven 'spokes', that of an adolescent in placement 12 'spokes'. It is thus obvious that much of the work of a placement will consist in promoting communication and avoiding misunderstandings.

The first difference between a 'normal' adolescent and a boy or girl in placement is the presence of social workers. The responsibilities of the divisional and project social workers,

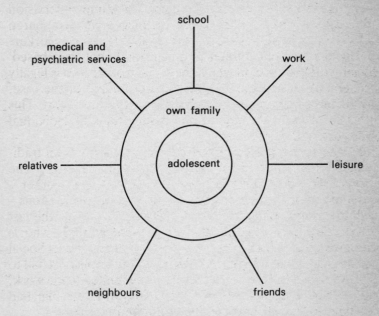

Figure 4.1
Social relationships of normal adolescent

and their relationships with the adolescents, have been discussed above.

It was the job of the placing worker to ensure that the relevant roles and tasks were understood and accepted by all concerned, and to check that the arrangements worked. This was generally the most time-consuming and possibly the most important part of the work, as the participants all had different interests and agreement could be difficult or impossible to achieve.

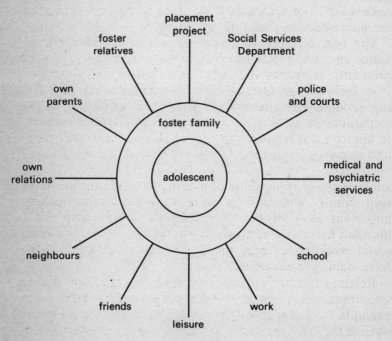

Figure 4.2
Social relationships of adolescent in placement

The adolescent usually resented having to see *any* social workers; the foster families had mixed feelings as did the families of origin. The adolescents had very varied relationships with their own parents. Some parents had died or disappeared; others had very close and loving relationships with their children. In most cases there were strong elements of ambivalence. The foster-families usually accepted without difficulty that working with the families of origin was part of the job for which they were paid, although in practice it was often far from easy. The foster-families operated from the adolescents' standpoint, however. They were responsible for their interests and could not take on other problems from which the families of origin may have been suffering – that was the task of the divisional social worker. This meant that it was often possible for a foster-family and the family of origin to develop quite a good working relationship for the sake of the adolescent in whose welfare they both had a stake.

The relationships of the adolescents with their uncles, aunts and other adult relatives did not usually present problems, but many teenagers in care had been separated from their siblings. Often they had been placed separately on the grounds that they did not get on with each other (separation being accepted rather than an effort being made to improve the relationship). Sometimes siblings had come into care at different times for different reasons and had never been brought together. It was considered important for the adolescent's growing sense of identity to be in touch with his own family, and siblings were regarded as particularly important, as ideally they would become helpful members of his adult friendship network. It was the task of the divisional social workers to trace the siblings and the task of the foster-family to encourage contact.

Relationships with relatives of the foster-family were also important. They could provide very positive help – for example, a foster-grandparent might act as a confidant outside the family or offer holidays or lodgings after 18. On the other hand, relatives were sometimes afraid of the effect of delinquent or disturbed adolescents on their own families and retained an attitude of distance or even hostility towards the foster-child, treating him differently from the other family members. These problems could usually be resolved, but some foster-families experienced some disillusionment about their own relatives' prejudices!

Both adolescents in placement and those living in their own homes had to learn to live in harmony with their neighbours –

not always easy! Adolescents in placement had the additional handicap that, as stigmatized newcomers, they were likely to be blamed if something went wrong. Making friends was also difficult for adolescents in placement, because they were often newcomers to an area where most children had grown up together and went to the same schools and youth clubs. In addition, adolescents needing placement are often insecure and low in self-esteem, so that they have great difficulty in making contact with their peers, either because they brag and show off or because they are withdrawn and timid. As most foster-families had children of their own, there was a ready-made link with other families, but some foster-families had to work hard to encourage peer-group friendships.

Developing friendships with friends and relatives is person-to-person work, which the foster-family could usually undertake without much outside help. Forming successful relationships with public services – the education system, the police and the courts, medical and psychiatric facilities, recreational and employment services – raised other issues.

The education system

All adolescents are legally required to attend school until they are 16 years of age, and many of them resent their last year or two of education and behave in disruptive and anti-social ways. The adolescents in placement often had a long history of truancy and school difficulties and, at the age of 14 or 15, not much time was available in which to put matters right.

As schools already had considerable difficulties with a substantial minority of their older boys and girls, it is not surprising that they sometimes objected to admitting a delinquent 15-year-old with an appalling school record. They were also fairly accustomed to the breakdown of traditional fostering following bad behaviour and were very conscious of the appalling results of moving a child from one family or institution to another, so that education as well as social living is disrupted. There is considerable evidence that children in care under-achieve in school and tend to move into unskilled employment.[6]

It was obviously important, therefore, to develop a partnership with the educational system. When the project was set up, a circular was sent out by the Chief Education Officer to the heads of all secondary schools in Kent. The circular pointed out that the project was a new venture and that as the foster-parents were paid workers, it was anticipated that they would play a very active role in promoting the education of the adolescents. It was constantly necessary to encourage the schools to make demands on the foster-parents, who were always willing to participate but did not always know what to do.

On the whole, very good partnerships were established between the foster-parents and the schools. Teachers were imaginative and flexible in helping the adolescents to catch up, and the school administration and the foster-parents collaborated closely to check truancy, as one of the foster-parents describes:

Pauline, aged 15, came to stay with us six months ago, having spent a year moving from one children's home to another and managing to run away from each in turn. One of the effects of this was that she had missed all of the fourth year of school.

Our local school is a large, modern comprehensive with approximately 300 pupils in the fifth year. Pauline had considerable difficulty in relating to all adults and a tendency to aggression if threatened in any way. We were therefore apprehensive about her prospects.

With Pauline's consent, we told the headmistress at the outset the problems we were facing, and she proved very sensitive and accepted Pauline immediately, giving her the choice of starting in the fourth year. Pauline felt that this would be a humiliating experience and that she would rather face the difficulties of catching up with her own age group. She was therefore placed in the fifth year.

The first few weeks proved to be very taxing on all sides. Pauline became disheartened on realizing exactly what problems she had set herself. She felt that as she could not take any exams at the end of the year, it was hardly worth putting in any effort. She therefore missed school at every opportunity and refused to wear uniform.

The organization and efficiency with which the school faced this difficulty was impressive. If Pauline missed registration, the secretary normally telephoned me within five minutes. At this point I felt that the school could have left the responsibility of Pauline's problems entirely to me, but they took a very keen interest and asked me to go for another interview. They offered to alter the timetable and allow Pauline to do private study and projects which interested her. They insisted that she did the basic subjects, English, maths, religious education and child care. Apart from these, she chose her projects and filled in the day working on them under supervision. As she was still left with free periods, the headmistress suggested that Pauline could help in the school office, filing, answering the telephone and manning the inquiry desk for short periods. Not only did this give Pauline a sense of responsibility, but her appearance immediately improved. We had further meetings to discuss a possible career. Hairdressing seemed to be the obvious choice. With this in mind, the school have told Pauline that if she maintains her improvement, they will try to get her a position as an assistant in a local hairdresser's on a day-release basis.

Admission to schools:
The most difficult manoeuvres were necessary at the start of a placement. Placement in the most suitable family often meant a change of secondary school and occasionally some choice was involved. The people whose opinions had to be taken into account when such decisions were made were the adolescent, the foster-parents, the natural parents, the divisional social worker, the project worker, the divisional education officer, the head of the former school, the head of the proposed school and the educational psychologist (occasionally). At the same time, these difficult manoeuvres had to be carried out fast, so that the adolescent was not temporarily excluded from school. The pivot was the divisional education officers, and it was very important to help them to understand how professional foster-parents should be treated – as colleagues on whom considerable demands could be made but who expected clear explanations.

On occasions, the project certainly failed to consult appropriately, and some schools colluded by simply admitting a boy or girl without further formalities. On other occasions, the Education Department had just cause for complaint – for example, when adolescents suddenly left school (because they had been arrested or admitted to a psychiatric hospital or for some other reason) and no official letter of explanation was sent or was received much later. In this area the bureaucratic formalities sometimes went wrong, but the face-to-face collaboration between foster-parents and school, with a very few exceptions, was extremely good. Foster-parents spent considerable time and trouble on discussions about choice of course, examination requirements and so on. And though teachers were not invited to attend six-monthly reviews as a matter of course, when important decisions were to be discussed, they were always prepared to come and offer constructive help.

Not very many adolescents stayed on at school for an extra year, either because they were glad to leave at the first possible moment or because a further year would only recapitulate work. No one achieved sixth-form grammar school standards, and only one proceeded to university. However, a substantial number of adolescents went on to technical college, where they successfully completed vocational courses of various kinds. The technical colleges were generally sympathetic and helpful when the applications were made, but in certain subjects demand greatly exceeded the supply of places, and the adolescents in placement were generally handicapped by a poor educational background.

Suspension and exclusion from school:
Several adolescents were placed who had already been excluded from school, but individual home tuition for up to ten hours per week was not difficult to obtain. This was regarded as only a temporary expedient, however, as it cut the adolescents off from the life of their peers. It was useful when only a few months of schooling were left or as an interim measure pending the availability of a suitable school place.

Kent had inadequate resources for the education of children with special needs. For those who were backward there were excellent day special schools, but for the emotionally maladjusted there was no day provision at all, except that one adolescent psychiatric unit provided education for its day patients. Thus if an adolescent was excluded from school on behavioural grounds, the outlook was bleak. There was a range of retreat centres and special units, but these only offered short-term help. There were educational facilities in a number of community homes, but these were available to residents only, not to local children, whether they were in care or not.

Suspension was less drastic than exclusion and could be regarded as an appropriate symbol of public disapproval. Some schools were much quicker to suspend than others, and some were more careful than others in specifying the exact grounds for their action. The project felt that both exclusion and suspension should always be supported by a written statement from the school, giving the reasons for its action and outlining the appeal procedure.

In conclusion, the work which needed to be done in relation to the education of adolescents in placement was complex and time-consuming. The foster-parents, it was felt, should generally undertake all face-to-face negotiations, but the social workers should use the evidence of difficulties to press for appropriate policy changes in order to develop a better system.

How the schools saw the adolescents:
A simple questionnaire was sent to the schools every six months. This was generally, but not always, carefully completed and returned. Of course, some adolescents were too old at placement to enter secondary schools or had only a very short period of compulsory education left, which was covered by individual tuition. Three girls were excluded from school and received individual tuition for some months (and there were 15 'false starts' – see p. 120). In the end reports were available on 53 of the 98 boys and girls who were placed under the age of 16. For some only one report was available, as they did not have very long at school; for the younger ones a series of reports was available.

The first and the single reports (numbering 53) have been considered together in the compilation of figure 4.3 (a)–(e) and the last of a series of reports – there were 23 of these – has been considered separately. The data are presented in figure 4.4 (a)–(e). The school was asked to indicate the class, stream or group in which the adolescent was placed, his/her attainment in relation to the class, his/her behaviour in

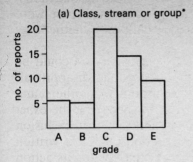

(a) Class, stream or group*

*Grammar school counted as A and ESN school or remedial class as D. Other definitions according to school criteria.

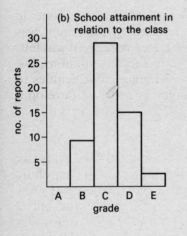

(b) School attainment in relation to the class

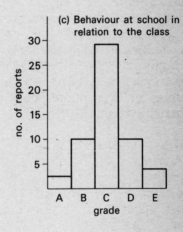

(c) Behaviour at school in relation to the class

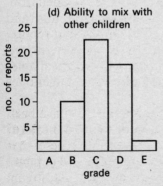

(d) Ability to mix with other children

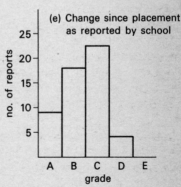

(e) Change since placement as reported by school

Figure 4.3
First and single school reports on project adolescents

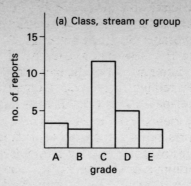

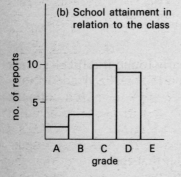

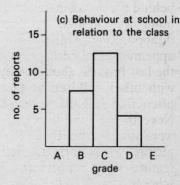

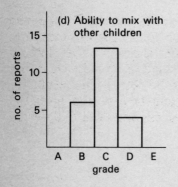

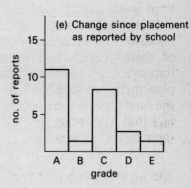

Figure 4.4
Last school reports on project adolescents

relation to the class and his/her ability to mix with other children. All assessments were based on a five-point scale: A – well above average; B – above average; C – average; D – below average; E – well below average. The schools also made various comments about changes, and these have been included if they related to the placements (if, for example, help from foster-parents had resulted in less acting out).

From the evidence certain conclusions may be drawn. First, the reports bore witness to a marked bias towards placement in the lower streams in the schools, which probably reflected educational retardation rather than lack of ability. Second, as far as attainment was concerned, the work was obviously hard for the adolescents, who were generally behind their classmates. Although the last reports show that none was graded E, the number of D gradings was disappointing. Third, the adolescents' behaviour at school appeared to be fairly normal, according to both the first and the last reports, though they clearly found it difficult to mix with other children at first (poorly socialized adolescents often find it hard to make their mark in a new school). Nevertheless, the last reports suggest that early difficulties were surmounted by and large, and figure 4.4 (d) reveals a picture that is fairly 'normal'. Finally, the most encouraging feature of the reports was the fact that the changes that the schools noticed in the adolescents since placement were very favourable on the whole – the foster-parents' interest and hard work clearly paid off.

Perhaps the most striking point was how little the adolescents' behaviour was perceived as different from that of their peers. Their attainments showed rather limited improvement, but the schools seemed to be quite clear that placement produced a change for the better. The results for the final reports were as good as could be expected, given the fact that most adolescents are restless and unsettled during their last year at school.

The juvenile justice system

The police:
It was obviously important for the social workers and

foster-families to have a satisfactory working relationship with the police. This was generally good at a face-to-face, interpersonal level and poor at a structural level. The one important exception was that adolescents were occasionally roughly handled by police. (However, on the whole, police are perhaps too amiable to adolescents, who ought to be rather frightened of them.) The police were involved in many situations resulting from running away, staying out late and misdemeanours such as drinking and fighting. Some of the adolescents in placement were a considerable nuisance to them as a result of behaviour which was annoying to the public rather than criminal.

It was both important and difficult to ensure that the police understood what the project was doing. In the early days there was a tendency to admit absconding or violent adolescents to residential institutions as emergencies rather than returning them to their foster-homes. Foster-parents expected to collect their charges and to work on sorting out the difficulties, and it was practically never helpful to remove the problem to another place.

On the whole, police were tolerant and helpful, although they sometimes confused adolescents by sympathizing with them in the cells and subsequently prosecuting them. However, the structural difficulties were complex and led to excessive delays in the hearing of cases and unnecessary public expenditure.

Kent police force has gradually been introducing a system of juvenile bureaux, so that during the life of the project this system operated in some police divisions but not in others. Where there was no juvenile bureau there was occasionally a lack of consultation between the police and the Social Services Department, which led to serious difficulties. Two examples will serve as illustrations. A boy of 14 with a long history of changes of residential care, described as being 'on the fringes of delinquency', was placed with a project family. A few days later a summons was received for the boy to appear at court the following week on a charge of being concerned with the theft of a bicycle 14 months before. The social worker was unaware that the case was still pending. The case seemed to upset the boy considerably, as he had just settled down to a 'fresh start'. Then a 15-year-old girl was placed in good faith, and the foster-parents (and the project worker) were surprised to discover that she was required to attend court on a charge of breaking a window six months before.

Where there is a juvenile bureau there is at least consultation in the shape of printed forms sent by the police to the Social Services Department and other interested parties, and there may or may not be further discussion. The juvenile bureau officer will then make a recommendation concerning prosecution or cautioning, which will be either accepted or rejected by the senior police officer. Such a system inevitably increases the time lag between the commission of an offence and the court hearing; even the formal caution takes place a considerable time after the commission of the offence. There seem to be many arguments in favour of the Hampshire system of an automatic and immediate caution, without consultation, for *all* first offenders and more careful inquiries only for persistent offenders.

A second cause of delay and unnecessary expense relates to the lack of co-ordination between the police divisions and the local juvenile courts. A concrete example will make this clear. A certain remand home takes about 30 boys for fairly short periods of time. The boys are upset and disturbed, as they face an uncertain future; as a result, they often abscond or commit offences in the locality. The home is situated mid-way between two small towns which belong to different police divisions and have separate juvenile courts. However, the boys' offences are distributed fairly equally between the two areas. A typical situation might be as follows.

John commits a burglary in town A on 1 June and further offences in town B on 8 June. On 8 August he is placed in a foster-home in his home area 35 miles away. The placement is delayed so that the court hearing for the offences in town B could be completed. About a week after placement a summons is received for the offences in town A. John, his foster-father, his solicitor and his social worker travel 70 miles for the hearing, but as an older boy who is now an adult is also concerned, the case cannot be completed. So another journey of 70 miles is necessary. John finally gets a conditional discharge. Seven months later John commits a serious offence while in foster-care. The hearing is local and quite prompt but cannot take into account the conditional discharge which was given in town A. More journeys?

Hearing all the offences at once is difficult to achieve but generally *not* impossible. Nevertheless, in 1979 one 14-year-old boy who was placed by the project with charges outstanding had to appear in three juvenile courts. The problem was certainly not yet resolved.

Finally, the present system appears deficient on several counts. First, only a selection of offenders are prosecuted, although 80 per cent of teenage boys are known to offend.[7] The way in which the selection is made is unclear. Second, punishment inflicted months or even a year after the commission of the offence loses its relevance. Third, prosecution of children who are already the subject of a care order is generally confusing, as the social services already possess far-reaching powers and there is often little or no action available to the magistrates. Fourth, a care order is a long-term coercive measure which is never reviewed by the court that makes it and against which there are in practice very few appeals. Adolescents perceive this as unjust by comparison with the determinate detention-centre sentence.

The arguments concerning justice or welfare are wide-ranging and are not the subject of this book. A study by Taylor, Lacey and Bracken of what they call 'our flawed system of juvenile justice' analyses the present situation.[8]

The courts:
The project became known to the courts partly by deliberate propaganda, such as the circulation of the *Annual Reports* or discussions with groups of magistrates, much more by the gradual infiltration into the courts of project foster-parents. This occurred at two points.

First, it was sometimes feasible to accept a referral from a social worker just before a boy or girl was to appear in a court case of which either a care order or a Borstal sentence was likely to be the outcome. It was then possible to set up a proposed placement and for the foster-parents to attend the court and to express their willingness to work with the boy or girl. Second, adolescents were prosecuted from time to time while they were in placement. The foster-parents were expected to prepare a report for the court and to appear there. They often spoke on the adolescents' behalf, and the magistrates and judges were favourably impressed by their commitment and perseverance. The courts very seldom refused to accept the project's recommendations, although they were extremely sceptical at the beginning!

Adolescents in project placements were almost always legally represented, so that they might appear in court with a lawyer, their parents, their foster-parents and a social worker, by contrast with other young people, who may appear with virtually no support at all. The project philosophy was that it was not the court's job to deal with trivial matters, so that all court appearances were treated very seriously.

Medical and psychiatric services
Any placement service has links with the medical profession in two ways; doctors act both as required referees for families wishing to act as foster-parents and as providers of medical care and treatment for the adolescents.

General practitioners as referees:
All foster-family applicants were asked to give permission in writing for the project to contact their general practitioner, to whom a letter was sent explaining the kind of placement to be made. Almost always the reply was clear and helpful. It was generally positive, but where there were reservations on grounds of health, the general practitioner usually consented to discuss these with the family, and an agreed solution was reached – for example, certain kinds of placement would be suitable but not others. On very rare occasions a family withdrew or postponed its application on medical advice. In a very small number of cases a general practitioner opposed placement and refused to disclose his reasons or to discuss the matter with the family. If the doctor concerned stated that his grounds for objections were not medical but undisclosed social grounds, the project worker made further inquiries and reached an independent decision. In one instance the project

proceeded to make two placements against the general practitioner's advice, and the outcome was very satisfactory.

The adolescent and the general practitioner:
The general practitioner was an important component in placement. Generally, the foster-family knew and trusted him and explained to him why they wanted a placement. In large practices and very small ones this was not always the case; in the former too many doctors were involved, and in the latter there was no choice if the family was not satisfied with the service they received. It was very important that a family should feel at ease in discussing placement problems with its general practitioner.

Apart from the care of minor ailments, the doctor had to carry out the adolescents' statutory medical examinations. In the case of girls, he had an important role to play in contraceptive counselling and (sometimes) advice concerning abortion. The general practitioner was also the gatekeeper to various services, such as psychiatric admissions. The extent of doctors' understanding of adolescent disturbance was variable, and on rare occasions misperception of the degree of upset could be dangerous. For example, one 16-year-old boy made a determined attempt on his own life and returned to his foster-home after a brief hospital admission. The foster-parents were sure that he would make another attempt, as they had not discovered the reasons for the first episode. The general practitioner visited, found no cause for alarm and refused to make a psychiatric referral. A second and nearly fatal suicide attempt followed.

General hospitals and out-patient clinics:
Adolescents in placement had the same health needs as any other boys and girls. In practice, they probably got a rather better service, as both the foster-parents and the social workers were ready to exert pressure on their behalf.

Psychiatric services:
There is an overall shortage of psychiatric provision in England, but adolescents between 14 and 17 years are in a particularly unfavourable position as out-patient services for children may consider them to be too old and the adult

psychiatric services may consider them too young. In this no-man's-land there are a few specialist services for adolescents.

Kent has two types of adolescent psychiatric unit. One type is based mainly on treatment by medication; the other relies on 'talking therapy', group work and work with the family of origin, with a limited use of drugs. The one unit of the second type accepts day patients in a separate section.

Nine girls and three boys were treated by psychiatrists on an out-patient basis. Four of these girls had previously been in a closed unit under heavy medication. In their foster-homes medication was either greatly reduced or totally eliminated under medical supervision. Two girls received psychotherapy; three were seen briefly for advice about specific situations. Two of the boys were seen several times, the other boy only in a situation of some danger. Two boys and one girl attended an adolescent psychiatric unit as day patients.

One boy and one girl attended an enuresis clinic. The treatment was completely successful for the boy but not for the girl.

Two boys and two girls were admitted briefly to psychiatric hospitals in situations of acute danger. One boy was admitted to a psychiatric unit on a long-term basis as a result of dangerously disturbed behaviour.

Help from psychiatrists was needed in two kinds of situation. First, help was needed in dangerous emergencies. Some adolescents who had been making steady progress for a long time suddenly 'exploded' for reasons which were, at the time of the incident, impossible to elucidate. One boy aged 16 had been in placement for almost two years without any untoward incidents. Suddenly he became very tense and chopped up all his possessions with an axe. The children of the family became very frightened, and it was felt he should be removed immediately. A psychiatrist saw him without delay and ruled out any onset of mental illness. However, neither psychiatric services nor the social services could offer a temporary secure place where his very acute problems could be carefully talked out.

Second, psychiatric help was needed with deep, on-going problems. It was the task of the foster-parents to deal with all problems and difficulties which were within the scope of normal parents or a common-sense approach. However, it was obvious that some adolescents suffered from very deep-rooted traumas and confusions which needed help from a skilled outsider. Sometimes this help could be provided by a social worker, but it was occasionally important to be able to call on psychiatric help. Because of the shortage of child psychiatrists, the project tried to keep referrals to a minimum.

There was considerable scope for developing the partnership between the psychiatric services and foster-families in order to provide an effective placement service for very disturbed children. Foster-parents would certainly have benefited from more opportunities to learn about emotional disturbance and mental illness.

Recreational services

Leisure pursuits outside the home:
The principle of normalization requires that adolescents in placement make use of the services generally available in the community rather than special services for client groups. The principle of individual placement, rather than 'like-with-like' placement, means separating delinquent, disturbed or deprived adolescents from other delinquent, disturbed or deprived boys and girls. On these two counts, adolescents in project placements were generally helped to join 'normal' youth clubs and organizations and were only rarely introduced to intermediate treatment activities designed solely for clients of Social Services Departments.

However, some adolescents in placement were so lacking in self-confidence or so bad at relating to their peer groups that normal social life was very difficult for them; occasionally, intermediate treatment activities geared to a group which was lacking in social skills were a very helpful resource.

Foster-parents were generally well-informed about local activities, and their own children helped to integrate the newcomers. However, many adolescents in placement preferred individual pursuits, such as fishing or riding, to group activities.

Adolescents met each other in pubs, and drinking was often a problem. Drugs were also taken intermittently, but the project had no serious problems of addiction.

Not all adolescents were interested in discos, but many were. Occasionally, attendance at discos led to staying out all night, drinking and drugs, but most foster-parents seemed to deal with these problems without too much difficulty.

Leisure at home:
Foster-parents repeatedly commented on the fact that adolescents in placement, by contrast with their own children, found it difficult to occupy themselves and quickly became bored. A few developed hobbies, but many equated leisure with the passive pursuits of watching television or listening to records. Many adolescents had very few personal possessions as a result of a poor home environment or of living in residential care. Foster-care offered good opportunities for developing interests without too much pressure – for example, cooking, helping with decorating or other household jobs or caring for animals, and adolescents often learned to share their foster-family's hobbies.

The world of work
Fostering means that adolescents can proceed from school to work in the same environment, whereas in residential care the practice is still widespread of moving an adolescent when he leaves school, so that the stress of a move and of starting work coincide.

Project foster-parents knew the district well, could liaise with employment services and were rather successful in helping the adolescents to find jobs. Nevertheless, throughout the life of the project unemployment was high in most of Kent due to the general economic recession. Boys and girls in care were generally under-educated and unsure of themselves. Their chances of getting good jobs were therefore generally poor and, in addition, many of them had difficulties with concentration and perseverance or had hostile feelings towards authority, so that they often found it difficult to keep a job once they found one. The various Government schemes to combat youth unemployment were invaluable. They offered the adolescents six months or one year of work at little cost to the employer, which enabled a number of them to gain a foothold in the adult world of work. Moreover, employers often showed themselves willing to respond to the challenge of helping the boys and girls in the project, even at some cost to themselves.

CONCLUSION

Maintaining and developing relationships with systems and organizations outside the family was the most time-consuming part of any placement. Roughly speaking, foster-families could undertake most of the face-to-face negotia'   with officials, doctors, teachers, police and othe   it was the task of the social workers to insist that th   opriate services or resources were made available   press for changes when the systems did not work. ial work has sometimes dodged this political challenge by tting up special services for its own clients, but this breaches the principle of normalization and separates the client from normal life in the community.

5   Outcomes and Gradings

Between May 1975 and the end of July 1979 156 adolescents were placed by the project, of whom 85 were boys and 71 girls. Their ages at placement are shown in table 5.1, the length of stay stipulated in their contracts in table 5.2 and the actual duration of the placements in table 5.3.

Table 5.1
Ages of project adolescents at placement

Age range	Boys	Girls	Total
Over 16 and under 18	32	23	55
Over 14 and under 16	51	47	98
Under 14 (special cases)*	2	1	3

*On three occasions we obtained special permission to place children under 14. Two of these were younger siblings of adolescents placed by the project; the third one was described by the superintendent of the assessment centre as needing 'more tolerance, patience, understanding, imagination and psychiatric skills than any child I've worked with in a long time'.

Table 5.2
Length of stay stipulated in contracts

Length of stay	Boys	Girls	Total
1 year or less	26	16	42
Over 1 year but under 2	35	24	59
Two years or over	16	30	46
Not completed: child did not settle/ placement too recent	8	1	9

Table 5.3
Actual duration of placements

Length of stay	Boys	Girls	Total
Under 1 year (total)	54	34	88
In placement on 1.8.79	21	13	34
Completed placements			54
Over 1 year and under 2 (total)	17	25	42
In placement on 1.8.79	5	12	17
Completed placements			25
Over 2 years (total)	14	12	26
In placement on 1.8.79	7	5	12
Completed placements			14

DURATION OF PLACEMENTS

'False starts'

Some of the boys and girls who spent a short time in placement never really entered the families and certainly did not commit themselves to the objectives of the placement. A period of two months was taken as a dividing line for those who failed to start. It was calculated from the date the fee was paid and ignored various 'coming-and-going' patterns. Fifteen adolescents failed to start, nine boys and six girls.

One boy was very institutionalized and did not like the stresses and freedoms of family living. Four 14-year-old boys showed a pattern of almost compulsive offending and absconding. They allowed their foster-families no opportunity to start any kind of relationship before the patience of the police was exhausted. Four older boys were placed in collaboration with the county's residential centre for remand cases. All were in considerable trouble with the law; either they continued to offend while other prosecutions were pending, or the court refused to leave them in the community.

One girl was placed on 'false pretences'. She had a record of attacking younger children, which was not revealed to the project. Her dangerous behaviour *vis-à-vis* the younger children in the foster-family brought her past behaviour to light, and she chose to return to her own family. Another girl began to settle well but left the foster-family under great pressure from her own family, to whom she returned, with disastrous results. Four girls never settled at all, showing violent, delinquent and very disturbed behaviour. Of these, one is now in a community home with education, one is in Borstal and two have 'disappeared', although one is known to be somewhere in London.

Of these adolescents, two girls and one (institutionalized) boy should have been placeable, given better preparation. The remaining 12 were probably impossible to maintain in open conditions at that time in their lives.

Placements completed in less than one year
Terminated placements of under one year's duration included the 15 'false starts'. If these are deducted from the total of completed placements (54), 39 'real' placements lasted less than one year, a figure fairly close to that for the intended length of placement (42). However, placements of less than one year include all the failures (all D and E placements; see p. 131) and some planned short-term successes. One example will serve to illustrate this type of placement.

Jean, aged 15, came into care in an atmosphere of high drama. She was in a state of open warfare with her parents; she had been arrested while drunk; and she had fallen out with her school. She refused to see her former boyfriend, preferring much older men.

She was placed with a young couple, both of whom were connected with the teaching profession and who had a very young family. Jean was not at all easy to live with, and the placement was stormy – but very effective. She was established in the A stream of another school and began to work hard. Away from her parents, she discovered that she loved them, and the family relationship rapidly improved. Her rather bizarre sexual activities were openly discussed at great length and gradually subsided. She returned to her original boyfriend. After four and a half months she returned to the care of her parents but still attended the new school, which meant lodging nearby from Monday to Friday. Her subsequent career has been very successful. 'A stitch in time saves nine' perhaps sums up this placement.

Placements which lasted for more than one year
Many of the placements which lasted between one and two years were of slightly older boys and girls, who were placed shortly before or after school leaving age. These placements helped with the difficult transition from school to work and worked towards establishing the adolescents as independent young adults.

The 26 boys and girls whose placements lasted for more than two years were obviously a younger age group. A high proportion of those placed at 14 years settled down in their foster-homes and wished for a renewal of their contract in order to remain there after the end of compulsory schooling, generally until they reached the age of 18. In these cases the foster-parents usually began to try to wean them into independent living from about 17 and a half years.

Transfers within the project
Transfers were moves from one project family to another. Cases in which an adolescent went home for a period and then returned to the same project foster-family were not counted as transfers. A total of 13 boys and 14 girls were transferred.

Some transfers took place because of changed circumstances in the foster-home. Two boys moved when their foster-father died and his widow had to give up the house. Two girls moved after a series of calamities broke up the foster-family. One girl chose to move to another family in Kent rather than accompany her foster-parents to a distant county following the foster-father's change of job. One girl and one boy moved when a foster-parent became ill. None of these transfers was unsuccessful, although the adolescents were upset by the events, and their progress was probably delayed.

Certain placements were mis-matches. It was not possible to predict accurately how an adolescent will interact with a family in the long run. After an enthusiastic start, several matches were clearly not viable, and a transfer was agreed. It was then much easier to work out what the adolescent wanted and needed, and all these transfers represented a step forward. Six girls and seven boys fell into this category.

The transfers of the other four girls and four boys were highly idiosyncratic. Two boys failed to settle in two placements each (one within a matter of weeks). Both were subsequently sentenced to Borstal, where they were in further trouble. The two other boys 'exploded' after a long peaceful period, were upset for a while and then settled down again. In both cases the reason for the upset was an intense and confused relationship with the first foster-mother. One of the girls was determined to make her life with horses and was transferred in accordance with her desires – but this did not solve her problems. Another girl, after 18 months in placement, fell out with her foster-parents and asked to go to another project family she knew. This was a successful move and seemed to be within the bounds of normal 17-year-old behaviour. Another girl was transferred because her foster-mother could not control her promiscuous behaviour. As soon as she had moved, her original boyfriend reappeared and she settled down again. The transfer was an unnecessary move, as it turned out.

The project was able to draw certain conclusions from the transfers. For younger foster-children transfers are usually disastrous as they form almost instant attachments and interpret change as rejection. This was not the case with adolescents. Situations could be talked out openly and changes proposed and agreed. A number of transfers quite clearly provided a step forward.

CONVICTIONS, ABSCONDING AND PREGNANCY AMONG THE ADOLESCENTS

Convictions during placement

Twenty-three boys and nine girls were cautioned or convicted during their placements. Of these, two boys and two girls were 'false starts' – their constant offending prevented the placement from becoming established. The situation for the others was as follows.

One girl received a caution for shoplifting (a first offence).

Five girls had one conviction each. Of these, two were convicted of shoplifting, a fairly 'normal' teenage event. The others were deeply disturbed girls who committed rather serious offences (a false alarm, assault on the police and taking and driving away of vehicles), and one girl had five convictions, all for assaults on the police. (This outburst happened after almost two years of successful placement.)

Of the girls who were convicted, three were 'normal' shoplifters, who did not appear to have offended again. Of the four deeply disturbed girls, two are now leading successful independent lives. One has been removed to residential care at the insistence of the court, and one is still in placement but very stormy.

One boy received a caution (a first offence). Twelve boys had one conviction each. This was usually for theft or traffic offences, but one boy was sent to a detention centre for getting drunk and brandishing a knife. Five boys had two convictions each. One of these failed in placement because of constant delinquency; another completed his placement but is now in prison. One boy is still in placement but is very unstable. The last boy ended his placement by being sent to a detention centre but is now living very successfully with his father. Two boys had three convictions each for taking and driving away vehicles and theft during placement. One of them changed completely when he obtained a congenial job and became engaged. He is now very steady and successful. The other boy has been living independently for a year, in friendly contact· with his foster-parents and without offending.

Compulsive delinquency could prevent the establishment of a placement. On the other hand, delinquency sometimes ceased for ever the moment the adolescent was placed. Between these two extremes a substantial number of boys and girls continued to offend – not surprisingly, as it had already become a habit with them. (In any case, where boys are concerned, Belson shows that 89 per cent of boys of all social classes admit to stealing, so it is fairly 'normal'.)[1]

Although placement did not prevent delinquency, it usually more or less contained it. Most offenders were fined and ordered to pay compensation. One boy received a community service order, and two were sent to detention centres and returned afterwards to their foster-homes. However, for one girl and four boys convictions brought the placements to a sad and premature close.

Absconding
Adolescents did run away from their foster-homes. Some were angry, following a confrontation with a foster-parent; some wanted to stay out with a boy or girl friend; some failed to return to their foster-homes because they were afraid of a rebuke for something they had done or were upset by trouble at school or family worries. Absconding *could* mean that they were unsettled in their foster-homes, but they did not generally run away simply in order to leave the placements, as they knew they had the right to ask for a transfer – although this was a difficult negotiation, requiring them to call a meeting of all concerned and to try to explain what they wanted. The statutory four weeks' notice was quite often given and then rescinded.

Absconding is always dangerous and a nuisance but, with the exception of a very small number of exceptionally disturbed boys and girls, it was not a serious problem.

Births and abortions
Five girls had already given birth when they were placed. One girl had had twins and had allowed them to be placed with a view to adoption. A second girl (now aged 15) consented to the adoption of her baby. One baby died before the girl was placed. One girl returned with her child to live with relatives after a brief placement, and another is now caring independently for her child, but near her foster-home. (There is some risk to these two babies with such young unmarried mothers.)

Six girls gave birth during placement. Three of them were pregnant before placement. Of these one consented to adoption, and two are now married and caring for their babies. Three girls became pregnant and gave birth during placement. One baby was born dead; one girl is caring for her baby in her foster-home; the other married but gave up the baby.

Three girls had abortions. Two were at a very early stage of pregnancy and appeared to cause little or no trauma to the girl. The third was a little later and had rather more impact, but the girl is now married and has a legitimate baby.

A foster-home seemed to be a good environment in which to work through very young girls' problems of pregnancy, birth and abortion.

THE ASSESSMENT OF PROGRESS

The Coopersmith inventory
From the start the project team was anxious to build in some objective tests of progress, but this was difficult to do without adding substantially to the costs of the enterprise, and no funds were available for an independent study. It was decided that a measure of the changes in self-esteem would be of considerable value and would be possible to administer by means of a simple questionnaire, to be filled in by the adolescent at six-monthly intervals. The Coopersmith inventory was chosen for this purpose and was administered during the life of the project. The younger adolescents raised no objections to it, but the older ones felt that the questions were inappropriate.

The use of this inventory, however, raised more questions than it answered. When the forms were removed from the files for scoring at the end of the project a large number was found to be missing, although in some cases the team member concerned could remember administering the questionnaire. Thus the data was too incomplete to merit a full analysis. However, the scores which *were* available raised a number of interesting issues. To those of us who knew the adolescents well, the scores reflected the difference between the boys and girls who seemed quite pleased with themselves and those who were more uncertain or withdrawn. However, what the tests did not show was whether these self-perceptions were reality-based or not. For example, three boys and one girl, whose careers had been quite disastrous, made very high scores, the most unstable boy of all scoring 90 per cent.

Where the trends of change could be established by a complete set of questionnaires, some boys and girls showed an upward movement in self-esteem which seemed quite realistic. For example, one boy at placement was physically frail and stooping, depressed and retarded. Two years later his health had improved; he stood upright; and he was self-possessed to the point of occasional insolence. The inventory scores exactly reflected these changes. On the other hand, it was possible for a downward trend to indicate progress towards reality. For example, one extremely disturbed boy, who had to be admitted briefly to a psychiatric hospital, made a very high score at the beginning of his placement, but at the end of it, when he had become a normal, independent young adult, his score was lower.

The conclusion which it seemed we should draw was that it would have been unwise to make deductions from the use of this questionnaire unless it was used in the context of other information. It was also difficult, with limited resources, to collect complete information of this kind – a similar difficulty was encountered in obtaining extra school reports.

Gradings in placement

Subjective gradings by the project team were made at the conclusion of placement or, for those currently in placement, on 1 August 1979. Assessments were made on a five-point scale: A – apparently happy, working or attending school, good progress with problems; B – generally positive but some areas of unsettlement/problems; C – no change (neither better nor worse than at placement); D – somewhat worse than at placement; E – disastrous. The grading for the 85 boys and 71 girls is shown in table 5.4.

Table 5.4
Grading of project adolescents

Grade	Boys	Girls
A	28	28
B	26	29
C	15	6
D	9	6
E	7	2

If the A and B grades are considered together, they represent a total of 57 girls and 54 boys (that is, a total of 111 placements out of 156 – 70 per cent) for whom the positive aspects of placement outweighed the negative. That is a surprisingly good figure.

The A-grade placements:
Among those given an A grading, 28 were girls and 28 boys, but two of the boys had been less than two months in placement, so they could only be described as having made a good start. In the case of the A placements the family and the adolescent suited each other and the adolescent was able and willing to work on his personal development.

Nevertheless, the gradings were fragile. When Dr Yelloly was carrying out her evaluation of 25 placements she visited a boy with a long delinquent record who had been living very successfully with a project family for two years.[2] The day before her visit the placement broke down in an extremely violent way. A turbulent period ensued before the boy was successfully re-placed. One day made the difference between an A and a D grade!

Reggie was an example of an A-grade placement. At the age of 14 Reggie was in an impossible situation. He loved his mother deeply but was in a state of open warfare with his stepfather. As a result, he had run away from home, been fostered without success and been placed in a fairly small children's home. He could not bear this limiting and restrictive way of living and ran away repeatedly, stealing vehicles, goods and money in order to survive on the run. He finally found himself remanded in custody as 'unruly'; at this point he was referred to the project and transferred to an assessment centre with a fairly rigid regime, including locked doors. He was introduced to a family living in the country with adolescent children of their own and decided instantly to go there. The first contract was for two years – that is, up to the end of compulsory schooling. Reggie attended school regularly, committed no offences and kept in touch with his own family. At 16 his contract was renewed for another two years and, with some initial help from the family he found a satisfying career for himself. His stepfather had now come to respect him, and the old wounds were healed. The final step was to leave the foster-home for independent living – a step that the family's own children were also taking at that time.

The B-grade placements:
The B grade meant that although on balance the placement had worked out in a positive way, there were fairly strong negative elements. Among the 29 girls and 26 boys who were given a B grading, one girl and one boy had been in placement under two months. Obviously, these two had not had time to settle down.

The B placements were characterised by several factors, some of which could overlap in a single placement. First, the match between family and adolescent was not quite right, but not bad enough to warrant the risk of a transfer. Second, the adolescent may not have been fully committed to change, so that the placement was reduced to a holding operation. Third, the problems could be so deep-rooted and pervasive that despite sincere efforts by all concerned, the situation remained somewhat unsatisfactory. Fourth, the placement was stormy because the adolescent was working through his problems; an excellent outcome sometimes lay in the future.

April, for example was a member of a large and law-abiding family but caught up in dissent between her parents. She was convicted for delinquent activities and placed in a hostel at the age of 15. Her behaviour, both at school and in the hostel, was difficult – she truanted, stayed out late, absconded and took drugs. In addition, she was depressed and on several occasions slashed herself badly.

She was pleased to go to a foster-home and became less depressed there, saying that she no longer needed to hurt herself, and she committed no further offences. However, she continued to stay out, discovered almost immediately that she was pregnant and was excluded from school on that account. She then became calmer and happier and built up a good relationship with her own mother – until she lost the baby. She then became restless again, running away for short periods and failing to work consistently. Her links with her own family weakened. She always claimed to be happy in the foster-home; everyone liked her; and she was pleasant to live with – but not really settled. She tried independent living close to the foster-home but did not like it. She then moved out of the area to take up a residential post and is now happily married.

This placement was constructive but not a total 'cure'.

The C-grade placements:
Of the 15 boys, two were recent placements, so that improvement could be anticipated. Four were 'false starts'. One of the others was very delinquent during his placement, but the boy's ability to relate to others and his relationships with his own family improved considerably. The placement ended with a detention centre sentence, after which the boy returned to live with his father. He is now happy and working and graded as an A outcome. The others did not appear to be either better or worse during or after placement, which was purely a holding operation.

Of the six girls, one was transferred to another family a few days before the date of the count (1 Aug. 79) and is now doing extremely well. Another was disturbed and violent during placement but has since lived independently, happy and employed, close to her foster-home. She is now married. A third girl formed only a superficial relationship with the family and was transferred just after the date of the count to another family whom she knew well so that the future is hopeful. A fourth remained extremely withdrawn after a year in placement; a fifth was just as disturbed after almost a year as she was at placement. The sixth girl survived a year in placement at a superficial level of adjustment, returned home and is now in prison.

Thus the C placements contained a fairly high proportion of placements which were simply holding operations and did not touch the real problems; on the other hand, some rather unsatisfactory placements could lead to a very good outcome.

Peter was an example of a C placement. He entered the project when he was just 15. He was the oldest of five children and, as his father had been in the regular army, he had moved about a great deal during his early years. His mother had suffered from bouts of psychiatric illness. When Peter's father left the forces he worked long hours to re-establish his family, but Peter roamed about, truanting from school and joining a band of youths who left a trail of vandalism and burglaries in the part of Kent where they lived. All were convicted, some receiving detention centre sentences, others being sent to Borstal. Peter, one of the youngest, was made the subject of a care order. Peter went first to a family which only had very young children. He said he was lonely and asked for a transfer. He was moved quite quickly to a family who had four children living at home, aged between 14 and 20. Peter liked this at first. He attended school regularly and got on quite well there. On leaving school, he started work at once and kept his job. He was never in any serious trouble with the police. However, within the family Peter did not do well. He made no effort to participate in family activities and was sullen and unco-operative when asked to do anything. The adolescents in the family began to resent him, and the parents felt frustrated. Peter complained that he did not like them. Finally, at 16 and a half it was agreed that he would return home, a few months earlier than planned. At home he was not very happy either but did not offend.

The D- and E-grade placements:
The D and E gradings included seven boys and four girls who failed to settle within two months (see 'False starts', p. 120). Of the remaining adolescents, three of the girls had long histories of very disturbed behaviour. One had a baby, which was subsequently adopted. The girl's time in foster-care did enable the adoption to be arranged, but otherwise had little or no effect on her. Two were unable to settle in their foster-homes or, up to the present, anywhere else. Their behaviour got slightly worse rather than better. However, a fourth girl, whose behaviour during the placement was very stormy, fell in love with a man considerably older than herself and changed dramatically. She was given permission to marry him, although she was well under 18 years of age. She married from her foster-home and so far the couple are very happy.

One of the boys presents a rather similar story. His behaviour in the foster-home rose to a crescendo of violence when he hit his foster-brother (an adult) and broke the front door. For some months subsequently his behaviour in residential care and lodgings was wild and uncontrolled. However, he is now living in a flat near his former foster-parents, visiting frequently, like a grown-up son of the family. One of the other boys showed signs of acute psychiatric disturbance and was admitted to hospital. One educationally backward, delinquent boy did not settle after three months and returned to his own family. One boy had only been in placement for a few months. He stole constantly, was very unpopular with his peer group and showed no remorse and no feelings for anyone; but the foster-parents will probably reach him in time.

Two of the remaining placements lasted several months and the rest were very short. All ended because of delinquency. Three boys remained in touch with their foster-parents from their community homes or Borstals.

The experience of Dick and Mary will serve as examples of D and E placements respectively.

Dick entered the project at the age of 14. He had been in care for many years, following the break-up of his parents' marriage, but always in institutional care – two years in an assessment centre, a long period in a community home with education and, finally, a period in a detention centre. He had thus never been to a normal secondary school and had a long list of convictions. He appeared very grown-up for 14. He was placed with a family who had a teenage son of their own and started school. He identified strongly with a teenage group whose members were expected to buy expensive and elaborate clothes and to participate in expensive group activities. He only managed to be accepted at 14 years of age because he was tall and a big spender – and, of course, the only way he could maintain this lifestyle was by theft. The family could find no way round this problem, and at the same time Dick began to dislike school and to truant, travelling far afield and having to be fetched back. Although he said he liked the family and there were flashes of responsiveness, all agreed that no progress was being made, and the boy himself felt he could not meet the project's expectations. He was transferred to another family and admitted to a particularly good school. Once again he stole, hiding knives and loot in a piano, although he also began to respond to the family and to enjoy the school. However, he was remanded in custody following fairly large-scale offences and received a Borstal sentence. Even there he was in trouble and was transferred to a stricter regime. He has written to his foster-mother.

Mary was placed at 16 years of age. She had been referred to the Child Guidance Clinic when she was of primary school age and, following a series of thefts, was received into care before she started at secondary school. Her parents were divorced but caring, and there was no obvious reason for her disturbed and anti-social behaviour. By the age of 14 she had failed to settle in children's homes and was admitted to a closed unit for girls, where her behaviour was controlled by means of tranquillizers and closed doors. School was available on the premises, but she made little progress and appeared to be of limited intelligence. She became very fat and masculine in appearance. At 16 she was transferred to a girls' hostel and, almost simultaneously, referred to the project. She found the new liberty at the hostel intoxicating, drank too much, became pregnant and stole vehicles. The police were anxious for her to be committed to Borstal. As a last resort a family placement was tried. She was placed with a rather dominant foster-mother, whose family worked a smallholding. Mary did not like it there. She did not work and continued to commit many offences. Despite heroic efforts by the family, she was sent to Borstal – which she herself wanted. It is difficult to see any hope in this story, but time will tell if this prognosis is too gloomy.

THE POST-PLACEMENT SITUATION

It is too soon to make any firm statements about progress after placement, but the following outcomes do suggest certain trends. By 1 August 1979 43 boys and 35 girls had completed their placements (excluding 'false starts'). The longest follow-up time was three and a half years, the shortest a few months.

We had no resources with which to carry out a systematic follow-up, so that the outcomes may not be wholly accurate. However, we believe that the general outline given below presents a true picture.

The boys

Twelve boys had returned home for periods of six months to three years. Only two of these returns were fully successful (that is, the boys were settled, happy and working). Three were not really happy and worked only intermittently but were not in any trouble. Two made a reasonable start, followed by disaster, and in five cases the return home was an almost unmitigated disaster (characterized by unhappiness, unemployment, offences).

Seventeen boys went into some form of independent living. Two entered the services (11 months and six months ago), and the first boy was delighted with this career, which was skilled. The rest, of which eight returns were very recent, found either lodgings or flats and were successful in obtaining and keeping work. Ten were happy and successful; three still had some problems and uncertainties but were surviving quite well. One boy had already offended again and seemed unlikely to break away permanently from delinquency, and another boy had not yet resolved his family problems. Most of these boys remained in close contact with their former foster-parents.

Three boys returned to their original residential institutions. One was being replaced by the project; one was starting an independent life in lodgings; the other had committed a series of offences but had maintained a friendly link with his foster-parents.

One boy had been admitted to psychiatric care and five to prison or Borstal. For these we felt that the long-term outlook was very bleak, although one of them maintained a close link with his foster-parents.

The picture for the boys had one particularly encouraging feature. Thirteen of the boys who had chosen to live independently of both their own families and their foster-families seemed to be happy and successful. Most of them maintained friendly contact with their foster-families, although for two of them this link was severed by the foster-father's death. Most of the boys were also in contact with their own families and seemed to have managed to find a satisfactory way of relating to two families.

There seemed to be a small group of boys who were

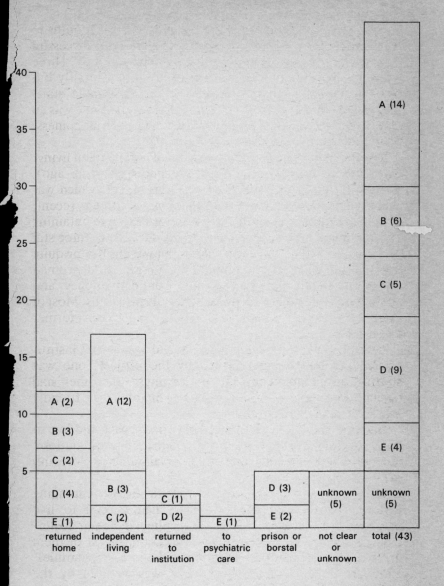

Figure 5.1
The boys: grading of outcomes

determined to pursue a delinquent career and could not be diverted. (This fact echoed the Swedish findings. Sweden has greatly reduced the use of residential care, but the country has a small group of adolescent boy offenders who appear to be untouched by any form of intervention.)

The girls
Only four girls returned home. One we believed to have been successful (three years after she left placement); one (ESN schizophrenic) was very unhappy three years after placement. We had no information about the other two.

Thirteen girls had been in either lodgings or flats for periods between six months and three years. They had been less successful on the whole than boys in the same situation. Two of them had been very successful; five of them had survived but had had a number of problems; for five of them the situation was unsettled; one outcome was unknown but was very unlikely to be successful.

Ten girls were married (only one of these marriages was very recent) and living in their own homes; half of these girls had a child. Eight of them were happy and settled; one was somewhat unsettled; and in one case there had been considerable problems. (No one can tell whether these very young marriages will last, but at the time of writing most of them were happy.)

Four girls had returned to residential care, two of them very recently. In one of the cases the project placement had been arranged as an assessment and planning period. After the girl's return to the division various disasters led to residential care, an unsatisfactory outcome. One girl among the recent returns had been happy and successful for almost two years in placement and was then removed, following a persistent and inexplicable series of attacks on the police. One girl was very unstable and did not settle in a family. The last girl was extremely institutionalized and never liked the stresses of 'open' living.

One girl went into her own flat after two and a half years in placement but committed offences, which led to a placement in a probation hostel, which she liked. She remained in contact with her foster-parents.

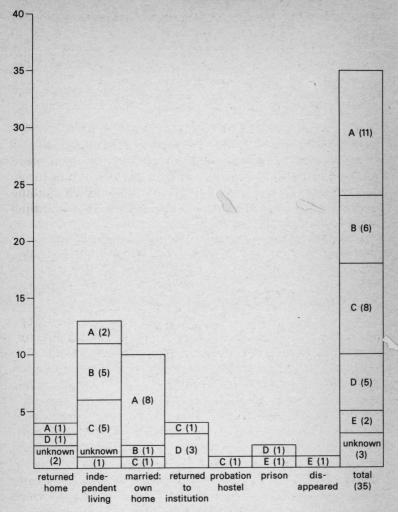

Figure 5.2
The girls: grading of outcomes

At the time of writing two girls were in prison. One had returned home after a fairly uneventful 12-month placement and had quickly developed a delinquent way of living. The other girl had left her placement, had gone to London and had been arrested. (In January 1980 she was back in the project).

One girl, who appeared to like her placement and her job, had disappeared without warning and had gone underground in London. Her problem had always been sexual promiscuity; it was felt that she would probably survive in the dangerous world in which she had chosen to live.

The post-placement pattern for the girls was quite different from that of the boys and appeared to reflect the cultural expectation that a girl's destiny is to become a wife and mother. The girls had been less successful than the boys at living independently, although they were generally very keen to start life in a place of their own. Early marriage clearly gave these deprived girls a sense of worth, of being loved and of security. They had tended to remain in contact with their foster-parents after marriage.

Relationship between grading in placement and outcome
An attempt was made to grade the outcomes as far as they were known on 1 August 1979 and to relate these gradings to the degree of success during placement. However, our knowledge of the outcomes was so sketchy that no firm conclusions could be drawn. As far as we could see, the situation seemed to be as follows.

There was no certainty that an A placement would lead to an A outcome. For example, a single isolated outburst could land a young person in prison. However, most A placement boys and girls seemed to do quite well subsequently.

The B placements seemed to lead to a wide scatter of outcomes. Some children were very successful; some survived; and some went to Borstal or prison. In other words, these rather uncertain placements could either pave the way for success or fail to solve the problems. Nevertheless, A and B outcomes seemed to predominate.

Some C placements were followed by very successful outcomes, but most of them seemed to lead to 'survival' and a few to disaster.

Most of the D and E boys and all the D and E girls were admitted to residential care or Borstal, although one boy whose placement had been graded as D returned to his parents with great success (A), another managed to survive at home, and one girl made a very successful marriage.

These outcomes, as far as we could tell, were more or less what could have been expected. Some stormy placements paved the way for subsequent success; occasionally, a promising boy or girl was suddenly upset, with disastrous results. The majority of 'good' placements probably led to successful outcomes. The most satisfactory outcomes were independent living for boys and early marriage for girls. More boys and girls might have been able to make a success of independent living if they had been able to obtain cheap rented accommodation.

The question of aftercare

However much adolescents improve during placement with foster-families, the money and effort will have been wasted if they revert to delinquency, unemployment and emotional disorders when they leave their foster-homes. (Clarke and Cornish estimated that residential care had a lasting impact on only about 20 per cent of the boys they studied.)[3] From the figures available in 1979, it looked as if the project would do considerably better; but this impression will never be confirmed unless a follow-up study is undertaken.

The indications are that a return to the family of origin in late adolescence is unpromising. On the other hand, independence is difficult – particularly in areas of high unemployment and where accommodation is scarce and expensive. The project's foster-parents have offered an excellent (unpaid) after-care service, but much more could be done, at relatively little cost, to help these young people to establish themselves.

Under Section 20 of the Children Act 1948 a local authority may make grants to people aged 18 to 21 who are in its care to enable them to continue their education, and under the Children and Young Persons Act 1963 a local authority may give financial help to young people 'in exceptional circumstances'. However, a survey carried out in 1978 by the advice agency for the single homeless in London, After Six, showed that only six out of 32 London boroughs had special allocations for young people coming out of care – and, of course, because such provisions are discretionary, they are an easy target for local authority cuts. The most disturbing feature of all is that there is no record of what happens to children after they leave care.

The most urgent change which is needed is for local councils to extend their housing to single young people. Girls with babies are usually quickly housed, but there is virtually nothing available for single boys. In addition, it would be possible to develop other ways of independent living. At present many residential establishments expect boys and girls to leave when they are 16 – just as they are starting work. At 18 years they are out of care, and social-work support generally ceases. There would be advantages in developing living groups which crossed these age divisions.

In Berlin 'living communites' (*Wohngemeinschaften*) have been developed for adolescents aged 15 to 20 years. Six to eight boys and girls live together in an ordinary house or flat. No staff live with them, but two part-time social workers are attached to the group and are available at any time. Their task is to help the group to learn to solve their own problems by themselves. If they run out of money, how will they eat? If the neighbours complain, what can they do? They must work all this out for themselves.

The group are introduced to each other in advance and must agree to attend school or work. Although the building is subsidized, all the residents must be self-supporting, by wages, social security or, for those still at school, by an allowance which they collect each week from the Social Services Department. The emphasis is on group living – if permanent pairs form, they are asked to leave. The age range means that the more stable older ones may be a help to the younger ones. Such groups combat the dependency which a life in care almost always creates. (In Berlin, by 1979, the first houses had been so successful that a further 200 places were planned.)

In conclusion, the project's post-placement situation is not yet clear but is certainly not disastrous. Undoubtedly, the success rate could be improved if there were more support available for the 17 to 21 age group. Such improvements would not be costly, and the money would be a good investment; young people seem to settle down in any case by the time they are 25, so that the risky period is relatively short.

6　The Problem of Evaluation

ASSESSMENT AND COMPARISON OF SIMILAR FOSTERING SCHEMES

The Kent project evaluation

The project tried to obtain funds for two studies: the first to assess improvement during placement; the second to assess improvement during a three-year post-placement period. By the end of the project we had had no success in arranging either. However, Kent Social Services Committee agreed to pay for a pilot study of 25 consecutive cases, which was carried out by Dr Margaret Yelloly, head of social work courses at Goldsmith College, London. Dr Yelloly was entirely independent of the project. Her study was published in 1979.[1]

Dr Yelloly sought to determine the degree of change in relation to specified behavioural problems or deficits which were described in the various reports available at the point of referral. As well as 'hard' data, such as employment record or convictions, she took into consideration the views of the adolescent, the foster-family, the divisional social worker and the project worker, but the available funds were insufficient to allow the natural parents to be included.

An evaluation of this kind is a difficult and complicated exercise, and Dr Yelloly makes the following reservation:

> What is being evaluated is not a single event but a dynamically changing and extremely complex situation; behaviour may change markedly before or after the precise point in time at which an interview takes place. For this reason the evaluation of placements still in progress is in my view questionable and

may be misleading: a follow-up after a clearly defined and consistent interval is obviously a crucial consideration for future evaluations. This was highlighted by my visit to one placement which had continued very successfully for nearly two years, but had come to grief in a dramatic and violent way in the week prior to my visit.

The overall assessment took into account changes in confidence, social skills and capacity for interpersonal relationships, as well as delinquent behaviour and other specific behaviour problems. The findings are shown in table 6.1. Divisional social workers, project social workers and foster-parents were asked to give the adolescents an overall rating. Those of the divisional social workers (though reached in a different way) accorded fairly closely with this assessment, but those of the project workers and foster-parents were rather higher.

Table 6.1
Adolescent change during period of placement
(evaluator's assessment)

Change in adolescent	No. of adolescents	%	
Benefited greatly	12	48	76
Benefited somewhat	7	28	
No apparent change/can't say	4	16	
Deteriorated somewhat	2	8	
Deteriorated greatly	0	0	
Totals	25	100	

Thus a central finding was that 76 per cent, or three-quarters of the adolescents, were considered to have benefited greatly or to some extent. Dr Yelloly adds a particularly interesting comment: 'While I assessed two adolescents as being rather worse during the time they were with the project than they were before, none was considered by any of the respondents to have deteriorated greatly or to have actually been harmed.' The main positive changes related to increases in self-esteem and self-confidence, social skills, practical skills for daily living, school or work progress and the ability to get on with others. It was not possible to assess how far placement actually prevented delinquency or stopped it.

Dr Yelloly points out how much work had gone into helping the boys and girls to come to terms with their family situation, but she also shows how few of the families of origin were really useful to the adolescents. In summary:

> Ten (40 per cent) had no contact with their family of origin; fifteen (60 per cent) had some contact. Of the 15 who did, four were no longer in touch and did not wish to be (in each case contact had been slight for years); eight maintained a strong link with their family of origin (at least monthly contact); and three maintained some or occasional contact but the relationship was poor.
>
> Thus in all 11 (44 per cent) had contact with their families of origin, but in all but three there was little likelihood of a home ever being available to them with a natural parent; such children have been aptly described as 'orphans of the living'.

During placement not a great deal of change in the adolescents' relationships with their family of origin was noted. *All* the foster-parents reported that the adolescents had problems in relation to their family of origin.

It was found that the placement of a second project child was often perilous for the first adolescent, who resented the newcomer. Role relationships within the foster-family also seemed to be far more confusing for an adolescent than for a younger child. The foster-parents were not 'parents' to him, yet the relationship was a close and intimate one. There was no accepted script for these roles. The report also pinpoints how difficult the sharing and consideration for others which are part of normal family living may be for adolescents whose only experience is of institutional care or abnormal family relationships. Finally, close and trusting relationships were frightening for youngsters who had learned to defend themselves against feelings for fear of being hurt.

In five cases Dr Yelloly felt that the match between adolescent and family was not right. In four of these cases the adolescent was transferred, but one remained and did well. On the whole, the divisional social workers expressed satisfaction with the placements – 80 per cent were considered very or reasonably suitable. Unfortunately, only 13 (52 per cent) of the adolescents were actually interviewed, but of these 10 rated the project as having been 'very helpful'.

The foster-parents were also generally satisfied with the job, and 68 per cent of them said that they would do it again. On the whole, the project adolescents established good relationships with the children of the foster-families. However, the impact of this kind of fostering on family life was considerable:

> One foster-mother commented that she and her husband could never go out together and that their social life was virtually non-existent as a result. Others mentioned the emotionally taxing nature of the work, which left them feeling drained and exhausted. Many of the foster-parents had devoted great thought and patience to helping the adolescent with his (usually) many problems and to thinking through how difficulties and crises could most constructively be handled as they arose, sometimes to the extent that their own children received less attention.

Seventy-five per cent of the families thought the groups were very useful or fairly useful. They appreciated being able to share problems and learning from other people's experiences and felt they could not have coped without them. Those who were critical either found the groups superficial or objected to the dominance of one or two foster-parents, who made them feel that they did not fit in. Only two families regarded the groups as not useful.

The families expressed a high level of satisfaction with the support given by the project workers. No family was either neutral or dissatisfied in relation to this service. Where the divisional social workers were concerned, responses ranged from 'very satisfied' (four families – 17 per cent) to very dissatisfied (eight families – 35 per cent). Dr Yelloly comments that these differences have a structural explanation:

In many cases there had been several changes of divisional social worker over the past three or four years, and one project adolescent had had some 12 social workers during the course of his life; the project staff had, however, remained the same, with the addition of one new member. Further, project staff had a specialist function and a limited caseload and provided a high level of commitment and professional support. All were of senior social worker status and very experienced, whereas some of the divisional social workers were trainees or comparatively inexperienced. The project staff therefore had some very obvious advantages.

In addition, Dr Yelloly describes the role conflicts already referred to on pp. 91–9.

The conclusions of this small survey were extremely encouraging and gave the Social Services Committee the confidence to extend this form of placement after the end of the project as part of the county's normal services:

> Almost two-thirds of the placements were successful, in that the placement was completed as planned (64 per cent) and three-quarters (76 per cent) of the adolescents were considered to have clearly benefited during the period of placement. Given the degree of social and emotional deprivation which these adolescents have experienced, a much more pessimistic conclusion might have been anticipated. . . . The resilience and adaptability of the adolescents in the Kent project was very striking, and although the past does shape perceptions and may leave lasting legacies, it is probable that social workers have tended to over-emphasize the traumatic effects of early experience. There are also strong forces in the present, in the living context, which make demands on the individual to which he has to respond and come to terms. A living situation with foster-parents who care genuinely but non-possessively and possess a good measure of insight, tolerance and ability to cope with withdrawn or aggressive behaviour may provide a good preparation for the kinds of situation likely to be experienced in the adult world.

The Hessen evaluation
It is interesting to compare these findings with the evaluation made early in 1975 of the professional foster-homes run by

the Hessen Welfare Services in Germany.[2] Their project closely resembled the Kent project, in that particularly difficult older children were placed for a fairly high fee. However, there were certain differences: a rather wider age range was accepted; there were no written contracts; all social work was taken over by the project team; a fortnightly counselling session with an independent expert was provided for all foster parents; generally, only families with professional qualifications were accepted, although exceptions could be made.

The last three points are important in relation to Kent. The Hessen scheme encountered difficulties in its relationship with the local youth offices who had referred the children. Taking over full responsibility for the social work did not seem to obviate these difficulties and certainly weakened the work with the family of origin.

The foster-families were critical of the expert consultants (psychologists and others), feeling that they failed to appreciate the realities of the job. Some families were beginning to set up their own groups for mutual support and help. Where exceptions to the qualifications rule had been made, the unqualified families seemed to be just as successful as the others.

The Hessen evaluation sought to differentiate between placements which were completed successfully and those which were prematurely terminated. The cases of 73 foster-children (41 boys and 32 girls) over 12 years of age were evaluated by means of a study of the files and a postal questionnaire.

Fifty-seven foster-children (78 per cent) were considered to have had 'successful' placements, as opposed to only 16 (22 per cent) 'unsuccessful' ones. This is a very similar finding to Dr Yelloly's figure of 76 per cent for those adolescents who had improved in placement.

The families of origin of these children were described as 'tense, unharmonious, aggressive and authoritarian', but these factors and other events in the child's previous history seem to have had no direct positive or negative influence on the outcome of a placement. Again, this echoes Dr Yelloly's words:

the decisive factors militating for a successful or unsuccessful placement thus seem to be grounded less in the personal and social environment of the individual foster-child *before* placement in foster-care than in the foster-child itself (which naturally must be seen in the context of its earlier environment and experience) and in the foster-home placement, as well as – and this is doubtless the most significant factor of all – in the reciprocal relation between the foster-child and foster-parent.

In the German scheme, unlike the Kent scheme, girls (and particularly older ones) were more likely to fail than boys. Presumably, cultural factors accounted for this difference. Although the child's behaviour prior to placement was not predictive of success or failure, behaviour *during* placement could be seen to be of predictive value. Certain forms of aggressive and unstable behaviour were markedly unfavourable, but 'deficits', such as contact inhibitions, some types of retardation and so on, seemed to exert no negative influence. In addition, the lack of behavioural positives could be as influential as the presence of negative behaviour.

Where the foster-parents were concerned, successful foster-parents took a child in because they loved and enjoyed children and were interested in child care as an alternative professional activity. The unsuccessful families were motivated by a 'socio-political commitment' – a desire 'to give a chance to the young', 'social awareness' – a somewhat theoretical basis for undertaking such work. The foster-parents' attitudes to child care which were associated with success were a 'generous and sharing relationship', 'emotional warmth', 'positive support' and 'raising a child to be self-reliant'. Attitudes correlated with failure were a 'cramping approach to child care', 'emotional distance', an 'over-critical attitude' and insistence on 'adaptation to private norms'. (However, positives and negatives in both child and foster-parents must always be taken into account and can cancel each other out.) Dr Yelloly comments:

All in all, it can be confidently stated that although individual characteristics both in the foster-child and in the foster-parents can offer predictive indications with regard to the outcome of a placement, it is more than probable that the final determinant of success lies in the reciprocal relationships between specific modes of behaviour in the foster-child and specific modes of behaviour in the foster-parents.

The Alberta Parent Counsellors' evaluation[3]

The Alberta scheme (described on pp. 24–5) also closely resembled the Kent project, except that the age range, from eight to 16 years, was wider. The evaluation took place after three years of programme experience. Its object was to determine whether the children had improved or changed and also whether certain characteristics and symptoms at admission could be associated with changes in functioning. In other words, did certain types of children change more than others during placement?

Sixty-two children were studied who had been placed in Parent Counsellor homes from January 1975 to October 1976. Of these, one group had been discharged from placement, and one group were still in the foster-homes. Standardized tests were administered to measure self-esteem, social and emotional adjustment and behavioural functioning. Social workers completed questionnaires at discharge and followed this up with three-monthly reports for nine months.

For those children still in placement the tests indicated a significant increase in self-esteem. The children became less distrustful, less angry and more controlled. They also became more responsible, more considerate and better at interpersonal relationships. However, the child's relationship with his family of origin did not change so frequently.

For those discharged from the programme the results showed less change, and the explanations for this difference offered in the report are all speculative. Sixty-five per cent of this group moved on to live in the community – in their own homes, group homes, in foster care or independently – and remained there for nine months at least. Nine children went on to residential care.

With regard to the particular characteristics of children which could be associated with change, boys changed significantly more than girls (echoes of the Hessen findings?).

Protestants also changed more than Catholics. Children who had experienced previous foster-placements changed less than those who had not. Children who had had school problems changed considerably – a very encouraging finding, given the hard work put in by the foster-parents in this area.

As in the Kent and Hessen evaluations, previous events such as absconding, delinquency or institutional experience were not predictive.

In general, this evaluation showed the same kind of positive gains as did the other studies. The restricted change in children who had had previous experience of foster-care did not accord with Kent findings – the adolescents frequently commented: 'Project fostering is different.' Whether the difference between Protestants and Catholics would apply in England or Germany is open to doubt.

It is interesting how closely the success rates seem to match each other. Dr Yelloly found that 76 per cent of the adolescents had improved in placement and the evaluation by the project team found an improvement rate of 71 per cent (or 78 per cent if the false starts are subtracted). Seventy-eight per cent of the placements studied in Hessen were successful. It looks as if about three-quarters of the adolescents in this type of placement are likely to improve.

THE PROJECT IN RELATION TO RESIDENTIAL CARE

The stability of the Kent project placements seems to compare favourably with the residential care system. Reinach and Roberts studied 65 children who had passed through a residential observation and assessment centre in 1973–74.[4] They found that on average each child experienced five new placements or changes of address (almost invariably residential placements) over the course of three years. Older children had more moves than younger ones; of the 36 aged 13 to 16 when assessed, 75 per cent had had four or more moves and only nine children were relatively stable.

Educationally, the adolescents placed by the project are very unlikely indeed to have fared worse than their counterparts in community homes with education. Early in 1980 a survey was published which had been carried out by inspectors of the Department of Education and Science in 21 community homes with education and which left nobody in any doubt that overall educational standards were a cause for concern.[5]

In particular, the report notes the inadequate use made of local authority support services; the lack of in-service training for teachers; the weak links between CHES and ordinary schools; the low priority given to careers education; the fragmentation of the curriculum; the absence of curriculum-development meetings; the underdevelopment of social education programmes; the *ad hoc* nature of the liaison between teaching and care staff; and the poor systems of classroom record-keeping. Malcolm Dean, writing in the *Guardian* on 12 March 1980, described it as 'the most damning education report of the decade'. The findings were not particularly surprising, as there is no reason to suppose that social work departments would be skilled in running schools. Furthermore, these units are so isolated from the educational mainstream that they have always had difficulty in attracting enough good teachers, although remedial education of this kind, dealing largely with school failures, ought to constitute an especially important challenge to educationists.

COSTS

From the outset, the project wished to prove that foster-care was a more effective way of 'treating' adolescents than residential care and would for that reason have preferred the two forms of care to cost exactly the same. In fact, the original fee was calculated on the basis of the minimum cost of a residential place for an adolescent – but such a place would have been in an ordinary children's home and thus not appropriate for adolescents who had been defined as having 'severe problems'. These would normally have been sent to specialized institutions, generally with education on the premises, which would obviously have been much more expensive.

Residential care and fostering: comparative costs (1978–79)

Residential care:
The average weekly cost of maintenance in a community home in Kent, with the child attending normal school, was over £100. The average weekly cost of maintenance in a community home with education on the premises was over £220.

Traditional boarding out:
The allowances for boarded-out children, which were tax-free, averaged out at £15 to £19 per week according to age for adolescents between 14 and 17 years. An initial clothing grant of £45 was payable, together with the following discretionary grants:

(1) Initial school outfit (up to £40).
(2) Extra clothing including uniforms for youth organisations (up to £30 per annum).
(3) Holiday grants and fare as appropriate, including holidays abroad.
(4) Extra boarding-out payments up to £15 per week (tax-free) at the discretion of the divisional director; amounts higher than that sum at the discretion of the area director. (The range of take-up for this extra boarding-out payment was between 30 per cent of children in one division and 2 per cent of children in another division.)
(5) Payments when the foster-child was in hospital.
(6) Supplementation of wages for working boys and girls.
Other discretionary grants could be made with the approval of the area director.

The rates paid often mean that the foster-parents were expected to 'top up' out of their own money – which residential staff were not expected to do. For example, calculations could be based on the National Price List used by local Social Security office staff in working out exceptional-need payments (set out in Appendix I of the 1977 edition of the *Supplementary Benefits Handbook*, the figures having been revised with effect from November 1979).

If adolescent boys wore men's sizes and girls of that age wore women's sizes, their initial clothing grant of £45 would only cover the items shown in table 6.2. Of course,

Table 6.2
The extent of the initial clothing allowance

Boys		Girls	
1 pair of shoes	10.50	1 pair of shoes	10.00
1 pair of trousers	10.50	1 skirt	7.50
1 anorak	16.00	1 raincoat	25.00
1 pair of pyjamas	7.00	1 brassière	3.00
1 pair of socks	0.85		
	£44.85		£45.50

adolescents generally had some clothing of their own, though often outgrown or unsuitable, and extra allowances were available, but they had to be requested and were not granted as of right.

Project placements:
Allowances for children placed by the project were exactly the same as those for children who were boarded out in the traditional way. Discretionary grants were also the same, except for the extra boarding-out payments, which were not applicable. A professional weekly fee (taxable) of £41.02 was paid to foster-parents and was increased to £44.87 from 1 July 1979.

Conclusions
On 31 March 1979 there were 2267 children in care in Kent (1200 Section 1 and Section 2 cases and 1067 care orders). Of this number, 1514 were in domiciliary accommodation boarded out, at home under supervision, in lodgings or in residential employment) and 753 were in residential establishments.

Traditional fostering, project fostering and residential care all require support services. In fact, there is probably more social-worker input in fostering than in residential care, and more in project fostering than in traditional fostering, but the input of work by the County Treasurer's department is probably greater for residential care than for either form of fostering. Thus the 'hidden' costs of different types of care probably cancel each other out.

Residential care is clearly very much more expensive than any kind of foster-care. Project fostering probably costs about half the price of a residential place for a 'high-problem' adolescent, but is more expensive than traditional foster-care. However the development of tax-free enhanced rates for special cases has narrowed the gap considerably. It would appear desirable to close this gap, so that a continuum of fostering careers is provided; each component should have a clear job description and should pay the rate for the job. This would range from an 'expenses only' payment with very little social-work intervention for traditional long-term 'substitute homes' to high payment and considerable support where foster-parents are expected to work with severe handicaps, psychiatric problems or extremely difficult home situations.

THE DEVELOPMENT OF SCHEMES SIMILAR TO THE KENT PROJECT

There is no evidence to show how much adolescents improve in residential care, and very little where foster care is concerned. Between the inception of the Kent project and January 1980 about 30 similar schemes were set up. In most cases very few adolescents were placed, few progress reports are available and outcomes are not yet clear.

Wakefield was one of the earliest schemes. It started in October 1976, and a progress report was published in December 1979.[6] The scheme is very similar to the Kent project but has interesting differences.

The age range is 12 to 18 years and, as in Kent, the placements are time-limited and contract-based. However, the families are assessed and selected by social workers rather than reaching their own decision, as in Kent. In Wakefield, as in Kent, one set of social workers works with the families, whereas each child has his own social worker. Contact with the families is carefully co-ordinated and very frequent, generally involving a weekly visit from one or other of the social workers. This is a higher ratio of visits than in Kent, where the objective of the social worker was to withdraw, although contact by telephone was always frequent. Finally, the Wakefield groups meet monthly, in contrast to the generally fortnightly meetings in Kent. In summary, the structure of the Wakefield scheme lays less emphasis on the foster-parents' assumption of the fullest possible responsibility for their own work and gives a more dominant role to the social worker.

In four years Wakefield recruited 18 families and placed 26 boys and girls. Of these three placements were terminated, eight placements were completed and 15 were in progress at the end of 1979. The report was cautious in assessing success: 'Success is hard to define and three years is a short time in which to evaluate a scheme.' Nevertheless, the general tone of the report was optimistic:

> All of the children in the foster-homes change. Their physical appearance improves; they grow in stature and confidence; most stop committing offences; and in varying degrees they begin to learn new values and something about family life to help them in the future. These kinds of change cannot be measured.
>
> Finally, a 'consumer viewpoint' from a boy nearly 18 who had spent two and a half years in a community school, followed by seven months in his foster-home. 'When it was offered I thought professional fostering was a soft option and I'd be able to do what I liked. I realize now that it's much harder being made to make your own decisions and having to learn to trust people and ask them to help you. It was easy in — school, as they told you what to do.' If he is just beginning to learn this kind of thing about himself, then we are not failing.

The Birmingham scheme for placing children over 10 who present problems and would otherwise require special residential care is an interesting variation of the Kent model. Between January 1977 and March 1980 19 families participated in the placement of 30 children. Of the 15 children who completed their placement, seven returned to their own families, three moved into a hostel and two returned to children's homes. There were three 'false starts'. It is now intended to extend the scheme to 60 families.

The particularly interesting characteristics of this scheme are its close links with the residential system and its behavioural approach.

The preparation sessions are held at the regional assessment centre and follow a deliberate pattern: they introduce groups to the basis of assessment (that is, the terms in which the social-work profession views children in care); how to handle adolescents and how to become accustomed to social workers and the system in which they work. At this stage useful ideas from behavioural approaches to child care and sometimes transactional analysis are introduced to the groups in as commonsense a way as possible. No attempt is made to dictate a behavioural approach, but the whole scheme is held to personify a particular behavioural method; the contracts are bargains struck on that basis and aim increasingly to incorporate elements of reward and sanction where appropriate as motiviation develops in the young person. Help from psychologists at the assessment centre is readily available. However, the behavioural approach is by no means rigid or mechanical, as the most highly valued and valuable response from any foster-parent in the scheme is thought to be his or her ability to react to difficult behaviour from a young person with a full and natural display of feeling but without conveying any sense of rejection of the youngster and ensuring that the child realizes the difference between rejection of behaviour and rejection of the person displaying the behaviour. To achieve this, it is felt that the foster-parents must feel the support of the rest of the scheme, its members and those servicing it; and it is in this respect that the 'tricks', devices and other resources of a large residential-care complex are felt to be so important and useful.[7]

Certainly, the Kent foster-parents found great difficulty in understanding the social workers' world and would have profited from better preparation in this respect. But is there a danger of turning spontaneous freelancers into pseudo-professionals by too much exposure to the received ideas of social work? The social workers' role in the Kent project appears to have been less dominant than in any of the other schemes, relying more heavily on self-help and self-determination on the part of the foster-parents.

It would be repetitious to describe all the schemes which have been set up or to refer to all their reports. Particularly interesting publications are Bradford Social Service Department's booklets which set out the differences between paid fostering for adolescents and traditional foster-care,[8] and Alison Mason's account of the work of the groups in the Cheshire Family Placement Project.[9]

If all the evaluative material from the various schemes is considered together, it looks as if the chances that adolescents will improve in placement are good. (As one of the Kent project boys said to a reporter: 'In the Home they taught you to play ping-pong, but here they teach you to get on with people.') The gains will be mainly in such areas as self-confidence and interpersonal relationships; there is less likelihood of change in their relationships with their family of origin.

However, evaluation as discussed in this chapter relates only to improvement during placement. If, as in the case of residential care, the benefits do not transfer after placement, the whole operation is of limited value. In spite of the lack of official support and housing for 18 to 20 year-olds, the project 'graduates' do not appear to be faring too badly. It is sad to have to repeat that we have been unable to obtain the funds for a follow-up study to demonstrate whether or not our optimism is ill-founded.

7 Conclusion

This book has sought to show that the traditional English method of placing disturbed and delinquent adolescents together in residential establishments on the like-with-like principle – same sex, same symptoms, same age – is expensive and counter-productive. English care and treatment policies for adolescents with severe problems seem to lead to the amplification of deviance[1] by labelling, processing and segregating the young persons concerned in such a way as to provide them with a formal deviant identity.

However, different policies in other countries show that it is not essential to use methods which segregate and set apart, and that policies which maintain disturbed and delinquent adolescents in the community do not appear to lead to public terror; they achieve results which are as good as or better than segregation policies for the same or less expenditure.

The Kent project was set up to demonstrate one way of keeping these adolescents in the community and of avoiding the build-up of interest in deviant behaviour which takes place in like-with-like placements. The project was an attempt to carry out a kind of 'action' research which, if successful, could immediately be translated into practice in other places; it was thus an attempt at innovation within the statutory social services. In fact, the model of a time-limited, semi-autonomous demonstration project seems to be a good vehicle for this purpose, as achieving change in a large, bureaucratized Social Services Department can otherwise be extremely difficult.

In January 1975 the project consisted of Nancy Hazel and a plan. There was a general atmosphere of scepticism and some outright hostility. It seemed quite likely that not a single family would be interested in this kind of work. Five years later the project had placed almost 200 boys and girls and had re-education than to the contemporary English lobby in favour of harsher penalties. If social control is to be exercised either by means of revenge, retaliation and punishment or by re-education, reparation and compensation, the project was on the side of re-education.

However, before extending a new method it must be shown to be worthwhile, or at any rate as good as the alternatives. How far adolescents improve during residential placements has never been satisfactorily demonstrated, but their progress after placement has been shown to be unsatisfactory in most instances. The project and other similar schemes have demonstrated an improvement rate of over 70 per cent during placement. Although such schemes have no follow-up data, there appears to be every justification for extending family placement while pressing for follow-up studies to be undertaken.

The development of family placements for adolescents is particularly important for those who fail to settle in residential care. If the articles which appear in the social-work press are representative of social-work practice, when adolescents behave badly in residential care the expectation is that they will be moved 'up the scale' – that is, to an establishment which is less open or more disciplined, or which provides psychiatric treatment.[2] The idea of reversing the process by seeking out a placement which is more individual-ized and less restrictive does not appear to be considered. And yet such adolescents often say that they want a family and, in the experience of the project, welcome what they perceive as 'freedom' and make constructive use of it.

The project method also challenged traditional practice in another way. Terry Bamford states: 'The main body of practice is still founded in the faith that personal change can be effected through a caring relationship.'[3] Yet the turnover of social workers is so great that adolescents may have eight or more social workers, may expect to change social worker each year (sometimes more often) and may even have had no social worker at all for months at a time. Most residential staff are just as transient. Given these realities, it is something of a confidence trick to encourage the development of a trusting and caring relationship, as harm caused by the let-down when the social worker withdraws may exceed the benefits mediated by the relationship. But foster-parents, who are generally buying their own houses, seldom move and do not change their caseload. This situation justifies the transfer of as many functions as possible to the foster-parents, particularly where deep feelings are involved, and leaves the social worker with the roles of organizer and monitor – very important but less personally satisfying.

Thus if family placement is to be extended, some means will have to be found of making fundamental changes in the way child placement is taught (or not taught!) in social-work education. The next step for the project will be to develop the travelling seminars which started in 1980, at which a project worker, a foster-parent and an adolescent 'graduate' present the project's methods in the context of overall placement policy.

The Kent project tried to establish whether family placements were suitable for *all* adolescents with severe problems. Some arsonists and some children with acute forms of mental illness needed more security and specialist help than a family could offer. Some very delinquent boys did not respond to family placements – but they did not seem to respond to anything else either. Certainly, there are no grounds for arguing that this form of care is more suitable for one kind of boy or girl than another. The transition to a family after a long period of institutionalization seemed more difficult than the transition from family to family, and the distinction between a 'treatment' placement and a 'substitute home' or sanctuary is crucial. Most adolescents were quite willing to try a family placement if the objectives of such a scheme were carefully explained to them.

However, English social work with adolescents is characterized by the use of coercive measures (care orders and so on) and of residential placements as a first or early resort, in spite of the evidence that these are both costly and counterproductive. The Swedish legislation passed in May 1980 provides that coercive measures (comparable with a care order) made because of an adolescent's unacceptable behaviour must be confirmed every six months, the social worker being required to show why a *compulsory* order is still needed. If this proof is not forthcoming, the order lapses. Swedish legislation also requires an independent scrutiny of the case of any child remaining in residential care for more than six months. Such changes would not be difficult to incorporate into English legislation if there was agreement that the use of coercive measures and residential placements should be reduced.

The extension of family placement is also important for reasons of another kind. The 'age of institutions' at its worst created isolated ghettoes for deviants, where like were placed with like. The public believed that the inmates were cared for by experts and felt absolved from further responsibility – and ignorance is bliss when control by drugs or brutal methods of restraint are practised. However, family placements keep the problems in the community and the Kent project appeared to elicit positive and responsible attitudes from the public. The placements worked as a system of mutual benefits. The creation of a new 'cottage industry' helped women to stay at home while earning and remaining professionally active. The linking of successful families with others who were in difficulties brought a new awareness of social problems and a new demand for better solutions – for example, informed criticism of the juvenile justice system often followed direct experience of the courts, and the experience of residential care was seen through the child's eyes. A crusading spirit on behalf of disadvantaged youth was engendered, the effects of which went far beyond the goals specified in the contracts. This sense of the importance of the work kept morale at a high level and gave all participants in the project the confidence publicly to state and stand by their views.

Notes

1 A NEW KIND OF FOSTER CARE

1 National Foster Care Association, *Education and Training in Foster Care*, London: NFCA, 1977.
2 V. N. George, *Foster Care*, London: Routledge, 1967.
3 The legal system in Scotland differs considerably from that of England and Wales, and the organization of the social services in Northern Ireland has quite a different history from the English pattern. For this reason facts and figures are given for England and Wales only, unless the contrary is stated. 'England' is used as shorthand for 'England and Wales' – with apologies to the Welsh.
4 D. V. Donnison and V. Chapman, *Social Policy and Administration*, London: Allen and Unwin, 1965, p. 27.
5 National Children's Bureau, *Highlight*, no. 6, 1973.
6 R. Jenkins, 'Long-term Fostering', Case Conference, vol. 15, no. 9, 1969.
7 G. Trasler, *In Place of Parents*, London: Routledge, 1964.
8 George, *Foster Care*.
9 Department of Health and Social Security, *Foster Care – A Guide to Practice*, London: HMSO, 1976.
10 P. Cawson, *Young Offenders in Care*, London: Department of Health and Social Security, Statistical and Research Division, 1978.
11 D. Thorpe, C. Green and D. Smith, 'Punishment and Welfare', Occasional Papers in Social Administration no. 4, University of Lancaster, 1980.
12 R. V. G. Clarke and D. B. Cornish, *Residential Care and its Effects on Delinquency*, London: HMSO, 1975.
13 S. Millham, R. Bullock and P. Cherrett, *After Grace Teeth*, London: Human Context, 1975.
14 S. Millham, *Locking Up Children*, Farnborough: Saxon House, 1978.
15 P. Cawson and M. Mardell, *Children Referred to Closed Units*, London: HMSO, 1979.

16 *New Approaches to Juvenile Crime*, Briefing Paper No. 3, January 1980. Obtainable from 169 Clapham Road, London, SW9 0PU.

17 Council of Europe, *Social Measures Regarding the Placing of Children in Community Homes and Foster Families*, Strasbourg, 1973.

18 A.-M. Duhrssen, *Heimkinder und Pflegekinder in ihrer Entwicklung*, Göttingen, Germany: Vandehoek and Ruprecht, 1972.

19 K. N. Hazel, 'Sweden – problems of plenty', *Social Work Today*, vol. 4, no. 16, November 1973.

20 A.-L. Kålvesten, *Caring for Children with Special Needs*, Marcinelle, Belgium: Institut Européen, 1976.

21 A. Rutherford, 'Decarceration of young offenders in Massachusetts', in N. Tutt (ed.), *Alternative Strategies for Coping with Crime*, Oxford: Blackwell, 1978.

22 L. Ohlin, 'Background evidence on de-institutionalisation and alternatives to incarceration', Lecture given at the National Institute for Social Work, London, 13 July 1979.

23 M. Bonhoeffer and P. Widemann, *Kinder in Ersatzfamilien*, Stuttgart, Germany: Ernst Klett, 1974.

24 A. Gassauer, G. Lehmann and I. Piorkowshi-Wuhr, 'Die Erziehungsstellen des Landeswohlfahrtsverbandes Hessen', Kassel, Germany, 1970. Unpublished.

25 P. Hamerski, 'Fostering a delinquent', *Adoption and Fostering*, no. 1, 1979.

26 R. Tozer, 'Treatment fostering', *Adoption and Fostering*, no. 1, 1979.

27 Alberta Parent Counsellors, seven volumes obtainable from Alberta Social Services, Seventh Street Plaza, 10030–107 Street, Edmonton, Alberta, Canada: vol. 1, *Recruitment – Conclusions and Recommendations*, 1976; vol. 2, *Recruitment – Appendices*, 1976; vol. 3, *Selection*, 1976; vol. 4, *Education Resource Material*, 1976; vol. 5, *Placement of Children*, 1976; vol. 6, *Casework Service Model*, 1977; vol. 7, *Evaluation – Outcome*, 1977.

28 Professional Association of Treatment Homes, 10279 Upper 196 Way West, Lakeville, Minnesota, 55044.

29 A. Kadushin, *Adopting Older Children*, New York: Columbia University Press, 1970.

30 K. Donley, *Older and Handicapped Children are Adoptable: The Spaulding Approach*, Michigan: Spaulding, 1975.

31 J. Triseliotis, *New Developments in Foster Care and Adoption*, London: Routledge, 1980, chs 10, 11 and 12.

2   QUESTIONS OF THEORY AND METHOD

1 R. Thorpe, 'The experiences of children and parents living apart: implications and guidelines for practice', in J. Triseliotis (ed.), *New Developments in Foster Care and Adoption*, London: Routledge, 1979.
2 R. Holman, 'The place of fostering in social work', *British Journal of Social Work*, vol. 5, no. 1, 1975.
3 Department of Health and Social Security, *Foster Care – A Guide to Practice*, London: HMSO, 1976.
4 Department of Health and Social Security, *Report of the Committee of Enquiry into the Care and Supervision Provided in Relation to Maria Colwell*, London: HMSO, 1974.
5 S. Millham, *Locking Up Children*, Farnborough: Saxon House, 1978.
6 H. N. Mischel and W. Mischel, *Readings in Personality*, New York: Holt, Rinehart and Winston, 1973, p. 163.
7 E. H. Erikson, *Identity, Youth and Crisis*, New York: Norton, 1968.
8 H. S. Sullivan, *Conceptions in Modern Psychiatry*, Washington DC: William Alanson White Foundation, 1947.
9 K. Keniston, *The Uncommitted Alienated Youth in American Society*, New York: Delta, 1960.
10 J. H. Flavell, *The Developmental Psychology of Jean Piaget*, New York: Van Nostrand, 1963.
11 J. Garbarino and U. Bronfenbrenner, 'The socialisation of moral judgement and behaviour in cross-cultural perspective', in T. Lickman (ed.), *Morality: A Handbook of Moral Development and Behavior*, New York: Winston, 1975.
12 Alberta Parent Counsellors, *Casework Service Model*, Edmonton, Alberta, 1977. For address, see ch. 1, n. 27.
13 C. H. Hagen, 'The contribution of social work to adoption', *Child Adoption*, no. 1, 1974.
14 W. J. Reid, *Task Centred Casework*, New York: Columbia University Press, 1972.
15 W. J. Reid and A. W. Shyne, *Brief and Extended Casework*, New York: Columbia University Press, 1969.
16 J. A. Walter, *Sent Away: A Study of Young Offenders in Care*, Farnborough: Saxon House, 1978.
17 V. N. George, *Foster Care*, London: Routledge, 1967.
18 P. Freire, *Cultural Action for Freedom*, London: Penguin, 1972; P. Freire, *Pedagogy of the Oppressed*, London: Penguin, 1972.
19 H. D. Kirk, Seminar at University of Exeter, 1969.
20 Hagen, 'The contribution of social work to adoption', p. 13.

21 R. V. Speck and C. L. Attineave, *Family Networks*, New York: Random House, 1974.

3   FAMILIES, ADOLESCENTS AND PLACEMENTS

1 R. Parker, *Decision in Child Care*, London: Allen and Unwin, 1966.
2 M. Yelloly, *Independent Evaluation of Twenty-Five Placements*, Maidstone: Kent County Council Social Services Department, 1979.
3 In a television interview, 1979.
4 A.-L. Kålvesten, *Caring for Children with Special Needs*, Marcinelle, Belgium: Institut Européen, 1976.
5 Kålvesten, *Caring for Children with Special Needs*.
6 A. Gassauer, G. Lehmann and I. Piorkowski-Wuhr, 'Die Erziehunsstellen des Landeswohlfahrtsverbandes Hessen'. Kassel, Germany, 1976. Unpublished.

4   OUTSIDE THE FAMILIES

1 A. Rutherford, 'Decarceration of young offenders in Massachusetts', in N. Tutt (ed.), *Alternative Strategies for Coping with Crime*, Oxford: Blackwell, 1978.
2 N. Hazel, 'Familienleben oder Institutionserziehung', *Materialen zur Heimerziehung*, no. 4, December 1979.
3 A.-L. Kålvesten, *Caring for Children with Special Needs*, Marcinelle, Belgium: Institut Européen, 1976.
4 A. Gassauer, G. Lehmann and I. Piorkowski-Wuhr, 'Die Erziehungstellen des Landeswohlfahrtsverbandes Hessen', Kassel, Germany, 1976. Unpublished.
5 National Children's Bureau, *Who Cares?*, London: NCB, 1977, p. 23.
6 J. Essen, L. Lambert and J. Head, 'School attainment of children who have been in care', *Child Health and Development*, vol. 2, 1976, pp. 339–57.
7 W. A. Belson, *Juvenile Theft: The Causal Factors*, London: Harper and Row, 1975.
8 L. Taylor, R. Lacey and D. Bracken, *In Whose Best Interest? The Unjust Treatment of Children in Courts and Institutions*, Nottingham: Cobden Trust and MIND, 1979.

5   OUTCOMES AND GRADINGS

1 W. A. Belson, *Juvenile Theft: The Causal Factors*, London: Harper and Row, 1975.
2 M. Yelloly, *Independent Evaluation of Twenty-Five Placements*, Maidstone: Kent County Council Social Services Department, 1979.
3 R. V. G. Clarke and D. B. Cornish, *Residential Care and its Effects on Delinquency*, London: HMSO, 1975.

6   THE PROBLEMS OF EVALUATION

1 M. Yelloly, *Independent Evaluation of Twenty-Five Placements*, Maidstone: Kent County Council Social Services Department, 1979.
2 A. Gassauer, G. Lehmann and I. Piorkowski-Wuhr, 'Die Erziehungstellen des Landeswohlfahrtsverbandes Hessen', Kassel, Germany, 1976. Unpublished.
3 Alberta Parent Counsellors, *Evaluation – Outcome*, Edmonton, Alberta: 1977. For address, see ch. 1, n. 27.
4 F. Reinach and G. Roberts, *Consequences*, Social Services Research and Intelligence Unit, Department of Social Studies, Milda. Burnaby Road, Portsmouth PO1 3AE, 1979.
5 HMI, Matters for Discussion series, *Community Homes with Education*, London: HMSO, 1980.
6 J. Westacott and M. Hemingbrough, *Professional Fostering – Just Good Practice?*, Wakefield: Metropolitan District Council Social Services Department, 1979.
7 Personal communication from Jim Clulee, senior social worker adoption and fostering, City of Birmingham Social Services Department, March 1980.
8 Bradford Metropolitan Council, *Facts on Fostering* and *Facts on Community Parents*, 1978.
9 A. Mason, 'Cheshire Family Placement Project', *Adoption and Fostering*, no. 3, 1980.

7   CONCLUSION

1 D. J. West and D. P. Farrington, *The Delinquent Way of Life*, London: Heinemann, 1977.

2 See C. Wright, 'What to do with Wayne', *Social Work Today*, vol. 10, no. 48, August 1979; M. Parry, 'Sheila . . . aged 15 . . . violent . . . wants to be loved', *Social Work Today*, vol. 11, no. 26, March 1980.
3 T. Bamford, 'Let's Build rather than Dream', *Community Care*, no. 315, June 1980.

Further Reading

BOOKS

A.-L. Kålvesten, *Caring for Children with Special Needs: A Study of 40 Swedish Foster Families*, Marcinelle, Belgium: Institut européen, 1976.

J. D. Cooper, *Patterns of Family Placement: Current Issues in Fostering and Adoption*, London: National Children's Bureau, 1978.

B. Kahan, *Growing Up in Care*, Oxford: Blackwell, 1979.

A. Morris, H. Giller, E. Szwed and H. Geach, *Justice for Children*, London: Macmillan, 1980.

J. R. Reid and L. Epstein, *Task-centred Practice*, New York: Columbia University Press, 1977.

Only available in German

M. Bonhoeffer and P. Widemann, *Kinder in Ersatzfamilien*, Stuttgart: Ernst Klett. A collection of papers on family placement, both theoretical and descriptive.

R. Plinke, I. Sell and H. Sell, *Erziehung in der Pflegefamilie*, Stuttgart: Klett-Cotta, 1979. A theoretical overview of fostering followed by a detailed study of the placement of a disturbed 11-year-old boy with 'professional' foster parents.

ARTICLES

K. N. Hazel, 'Children in Care should be in Transit', *Community Care*, 5 July 1978.

P. Hamerski, 'Fostering a Delinquent', *Adoption and Fostering*, no. 1 of 1979. The experience of a German family.

A. Mason, 'Cheshire Family Placement Project', *Adoption and Fostering*, no. 3 of 1980. Interesting comments on the Kent model.

Index